F

Christmas, 1992

Here's wishing seeing
through the big
fix-it with you —
Love, Phyllis

THE
BIG
FIX-UP

How to Renovate Your Home Without Losing Your Shirt

Stephen M. Pollan & Mark Levine

A FIRESIDE BOOK

Published by Simon & Schuster

New York   London   Toronto   Sydney   Tokyo   Singapore

F

FIRESIDE
Simon & Schuster Building
Rockefeller Center
1230 Avenue of the Americas
New York, New York   10020

Copyright © 1992 by Stephen M. Pollan

DESIGNED BY BARBARA MARKS
Manufactured in the United States of
America

10 9 8 7 6 5 4 3 2 1

Library of Congress Cataloging-in-
Publication Data is available.

ISBN: 0-671-76041-6

Information in tables on pages 42–56,
57–63, and 167 used by permission of
R. S. Means Company, Inc.

ACKNOWLEDGMENTS

The authors would like to express their appreciation and gratitude to: Shannon Carney, Gabrielle Kleinman, and Jane Morrow for their skill and assistance; Stuart Krichevsky for his guidance and encouragement; master builders Dinyar Wadia, Ellen Burcroff and Robert Anderson, Deborah Harkins (assistant managing editor of *New York*), real estate attorneys Mitchell B. Stern and Erwin Schustak, Howard Chandler (senior engineer/editor of the R.S. Means Company), real estate appraiser and broker George DeVoe, construction manager Robert Cucullo of C.M. Roberts, Inc. and Steven Heller of Cardinal Properties, and Joseph Provey (former editor of *Practical Homeowner*) for their input and advice; Ed Walters for his patience and confidence; and most of all Corky Pollan and Deirdre Levine for their support and love.

CONTENTS

Introduction

This is probably the only home renovation book written by someone who doesn't know how to hammer a nail. Actually, I do know how . . . I just don't do it for a living. What I do is advise people on, and write about, the business of living. That's a term I use to describe all of the multifaceted, legal, consumer, career, and financial matters we need to deal with in the daily operation of our lives, including having renovations done to our homes. One of the things I've always stressed is that, while we need to be proactive and to take charge of our own lives, there are some things better left to experts.

In both my personal and business lives I frequently turn to others for the skill and expertise I lack. I don't feel I need to be an expert on everything in order to be successful in life or business. If my clients ask me a question I can't answer, or need advice in an area I'm not familiar or current with, I don't hesitate to reach out to experts for the information, or to send my clients to them. I think my willingness to admit my own shortcomings was a gift from my parents. They taught me there was no shame in not knowing something. The shame, they explained to me, was in not admitting you don't know it.

I'm especially grateful for this gift, because as each day passes it's clearer to me how rare it is. For some reason most people have a fear of putting themselves in the hands of others. It's understandable to some extent. No one is as concerned with our health, our career, our family, our money, or our home as we are. Yet at some point we need to realize that if we aren't qualified to do something we should turn to someone who is.

Nowhere is this unwillingness to delegate more pronounced than in the home renovation process. I've been involved with literally hundreds of renovation projects, ranging from the complete remodeling of a multimillion dollar estate to the face-lift of a studio apartment. As a real estate entrepreneur I built office buildings and small factories. As a banker I financed many residential and commercial construction projects. Since I've been in private practice I've helped clients calculate what they can afford, select and hire architects and designers, choose contractors, remove mechanics liens, and arrange financing. And, unfortunately, I've also on occasion had to resolve bitter disputes between clients and contractors. I've gone through five renovations of my own: the complete rebuilding of my vacation home on Martha's Vineyard; the remodeling of my Manhattan office; the restoration of my farmhouse in Connecticut; the total reconstruction of a guest house on my farm; and the reconditioning of a gate house on the same property.

Through all these renovations I've come to realize there's so much time and energy involved in just being a smart homeowner—in deciding whether or not to renovate and what to have done, in calculating how much you can afford to spend, in selecting and supervising designers and contractors—that it's foolish either to try to do the work yourself or serve as your own general contractor. I believe the best way to minimize the potential problems, and insure your renovation brings you emotional and financial satisfaction, is to leave it to the professionals.

But while the shelves of bookstores are filled with books written to teach you how to do your own home renovations, or how to be your own general contractor, there's nothing out there that explains how to be the most aware, sophisticated, and powerful homeowner you can be. That's why this book was written. It tells you what you need to know to: decide whether or not it makes sense to renovate; calculate how much you can afford to spend; select a designer and oversee the drawing of plans and specifications; and choose and work with a general contractor. It provides the knowledge, tools, and tactics needed to become a savvy home renovation consumer.

—Stephen M. Pollan

CHAPTER 1

The Case Against
Doing It Yourself

——

*The best executive is the one who has
sense enough to pick good men to do
what he wants done and self-restraint
enough to keep from meddling with
them while they do it.*
—THEODORE ROOSEVELT

For most people, their home
—whether a co-op apart-
ment, a suburban split-level, or a sprawling ranch—is their
single biggest financial investment. The equity you have in
your home can fund retirement, the education of children,
or provide seed money for a business. Therefore, anything
you do to your home is important. An amateurish renovation, one that's professionally done but poorly thought out,
or even one that is just a little too obvious, detracts dramatically from the value of a home and makes it much
more difficult to sell. You may think it doesn't matter what
you do to your home, because you'll never sell it. But I

must tell you: In my experience, every home is eventually sold, often much sooner than was anticipated. Even if this is the home you're going to die in, your survivors may need to sell it.

And despite what the other how-to books, genial television hosts, or the reassuring clerks at the home center say, you won't be able to do as good a job on your own. No book can give you the expertise and experience an electrician has acquired in thirty years of working on wiring. And no amount of previous business management skill or well-intended advice can give you the knowledge necessary to coordinate, schedule, and manage a construction job.

Americans have an almost innate urge to be self-reliant. Our nation was founded by rugged individualists, stalwart souls who struggled on their own against the elements. Our finest works of literature and most profound philosophers celebrate the independent man and woman as the ideal. It's understandable. After all, our forefathers crossed oceans in search of freedom and set out in wagons to conquer the frontier. Alone, or in small groups, with nothing but an axe and a rifle, they strived to carve a nation out of wilderness.

Yet even as the frontier vanished and our society matured, we retained this streak of self-reliance. And when it was no longer necessary to build your own home, or grow your own food, or defend yourself against outlaws, the urge for independence began to be expressed in different ways. Some of these manifestations were, and remain, powerful forces for the betterment of our lives. The urge for self-reliance probably accounts for our becoming a nation of entrepreneurs and inventors, a beacon of democracy, and the wealthiest and most powerful country in the world.

But there's also a dark side to self-reliance. We've somehow internalized the notion that delegating authority to others, or hiring others to do things for us, is a sign of weakness; it's almost un-American. People buy kits to help them write their own wills, rather than turn to a lawyer, even though the savings is minimal and the potential for disaster is great. Regardless of how complex and arcane the tax codes become, some of us stubbornly continue to prepare our own income tax returns. When faced with an opportunity to delegate some task to a specialist, many of us still instinctively say, "I'd rather do it myself." It doesn't matter if we don't have the expertise or skill to do the task in question. We still think we can do almost anything, if we set our minds to it.

A TOOL BELT DOES NOT A CARPENTER MAKE

While I hate to throw cold water on this deeply held national misconception, I must. Because nowhere is the fool-ishness of such an attitude more apparent than in home renovations. While almost all of us realize we can't do the job of an architect, everyone, regardless of whether they know the difference between a circular saw and a sabre saw, thinks they're able either to do construction work themselves, or at the very least, manage a construction job. Nearly every man who has hung a shelf thinks he can build a deck. Don't get me wrong, this isn't just a case of excessive machismo. While men are probably worse in this regard, women can be just as foolish. While she may not have delusions of grandeur revolving around hammers and nails, the woman who has successfully started and managed her own company often thinks managing a minor renovation project will be a piece of cake.

Our lack of respect for people who work with their hands contributes to this misconception. We're able to concede we can't replace an architect because they have an extensive formal education. But we assume there's some sort of strange imbalance between physical and mental skills. If someone is a skilled carpenter they won't be too smart, or at least they won't be educated. We fail to realize that just as much learning goes into becoming a good carpenter or a general contractor as a business person—maybe even more. We forget there are many fields in which success requires physical skill as well as intellect—surgery, to name just one.

We think, being well educated, that all we need to do to be able to remodel a bathroom is pick up a how-to book and make a trip to the hardware store, or call in a plumber, painter, and tile layer. Entire industries have sprung up to fuel this misconception. Home centers, hardware stores, and yes, writers of how-to books, encourage people to believe they can do things themselves. The do-it-yourself industry will do anything to convince a customer they can actually do a good job. They'll play on the popular image of general contractors as crooks. They'll have former subcontractors on staff to give "expert" advice. (If they really were experts they'd still be working in the trade—not selling products to amateurs.) There's even a subtle, almost subliminal message: If you don't do it yourself, there's something wrong with you.

Our childhoods also contribute to the misconception. As infants we quickly graduate from rattles to blocks. Soon after we graduate to Lego blocks or Lincoln Logs. We build sand castles at the beach. And while boys may have been socialized to deal with the rougher aspects of construction—toy tools and miniature bulldozers—girls too learn about renovation early. Dollhouses are built, and renovated. Toy appliances—rightly or wrongly—cultivate an interest in the kitchen. A boy who plays with plastic circular saws, and a girl who has a Suzy Homemaker

Oven, eventually grow older, marry, and think they can plan and build their own new kitchen. I don't think we ever lose this attraction to building. When I was a banker I loved putting a hard hat on and visiting a borrower's construction site. It made me feel—adult. To this day I can't walk by a construction project without looking through the peepholes in the temporary walls—and I'm never the only one taking a peek.

Lack of actual skill isn't the only obstacle to doing it yourself. Those who think they should do home renovation work themselves often fail to realize there's an added cost involved: their time. Most of us fail to account for our time properly. If you earn forty dollars an hour, you really *save* money by paying a contractor thirty dollars an hour to do renovation work for you. And even if you won't be taking time away from your job to do the work yourself, you'll be taking time away from your home life. If you're like me, your leisure hours are precious. Why spend them banging nails when you could be playing with the children, talking to your significant other, walking along the beach, reading a book, or even watching a football game. Serious renovation work is not relaxing. It's not like building a spice rack. You can't stop in the middle of replacing a toilet. If you screw up the spice rack it's no big deal. Screw up the installation of a toilet and you're in trouble.

A young trial lawyer who is an associate of mine decided to take an active role in the renovation of his new home. He and his wife decided they wanted their dining room and living room walls to be covered with horizontal pine paneling. Since the panels fit together with tongues and grooves, the young lawyer thought it would be a simple matter for him to do the work himself. Everything went along fine until he got close to the ceiling, or to a corner. He couldn't seem to get the panels on different walls to line up, and there was a huge gap between the top panel and the ceiling. In the end he had to hire a carpenter to come in and cover up his mistakes with very large cornice and corner moldings. And the painter had to spend twice as much time as would have been necessary, because she had to fill and cover up nail heads, splits, and hammer rings (which he now knows professionals call "elephant prints").

OFFICE SKILLS DON'T TRANSLATE TO THE CONSTRUCTION SITE

Even if we can admit to ourselves we don't have the skill or time to actually do the work involved in a home renovation project, we think we're perfectly capable of *managing* the job. After all, what does a general contractor do, we ask ourselves. You don't see any physical evidence of their work when the job is done. All you'll have to show for their efforts is a huge bill. Why not eliminate the middle man, we think, hire the subcontractors on our own, and save a bundle of money.

One client of mine, a very bright young man who edits a national magazine, was convinced he could manage the renovation of his own home. He even took time off work to do it. He hired a carpenter who was more of a craftsman than a manager, and an architect whose plans were magnificent but nearly impossible to build. The carpenter, anxious to get the work, never told my client he couldn't understand the architect's plans. And the architect, glad to have a contractor he could dominate, backed the carpenter in every situation. Needless to say the job came in way over budget and schedule.

While I think it's admirable to want to do these things yourself, you need to understand that doing work yourself, or acting as your own general contractor, is usually a big mistake. There's nothing wrong with indulging the urge to tinker or build. The act of creation—whether it's writing books or building a case to hold them—is invigorating and rewarding. And if you think you'll get pleasure or satisfaction from managing a renovation job, that's wonderful. Just make sure you're supervising the renovation of a dollhouse or a doghouse, not your own house. That way you can exercise job management skills on the weekend, and if you mess up the only one to suffer will be Barbie or Rover.

Sure, job management looks simple. After all, what's involved in redoing a bathroom? You hire a plumber and a tile layer and it's done. Or so you may think. Who's going to remove the old fixtures or rip up the old tiles? Who comes in first, the plumber or the tile layer? What happens if the plumber has to cut a new hole in the wall for a pipe—who's going to repair it? What if, after the old tiles are removed, it's discovered the subfloor needs to be replaced? What do you do if the building inspector doesn't arrive when scheduled? And not the least of it, who's going to clean up the mess after the subcontractors are done? With today's increased environmental awareness it's not easy getting rid of construction debris.

Houses are like heads of lettuce: multi-layered. You never know what lies beneath the surface—even if you have blueprints—until you start peeling it away. All the systems and subsystems in a house are interconnected: the plumbing and electrical wiring run through the walls and floors and ceilings, which hang from beams and studs, which rest on sills, which sit on a foundation. And there's no single tradesperson who works on every one of these systems. An electrician doesn't know carpentry, and a plumber doesn't know masonry—even though they may think they do.

If the tile layer finds you need a new subfloor, she's not going to install it. Nor should she. She hasn't been trained for it and that's not what she's paid for. Hopefully, she'll tell you to call in a carpenter, and then you'll have to call her back when the job is done. Meanwhile, the plumber won't be able to install the claw-foot tub or the new vanity until the floor is done. Of course you'll need to pay for the time they've already spent on the job. And by the time you find a carpenter and they install a new subfloor, the tile layer and the plumber will have moved on to another job. Since you're a one-time customer for them, you have no leverage. A general contractor, on the other hand, offers a steady source of work for a subcontractor, and therefore has the leverage needed to get them to come back when, and if, necessary.

LEAVE IT TO THE PROS

Since even the most minor home renovation job has the potential to be complicated and perplexing, I recommend you leave the selection, scheduling, and coordination of the trades to a general contractor, and not try to manage the job yourself. While you may never see physical evidence of the work done by a general contractor, you'll certainly see evidence if you don't hire one: It will be your out-of-commission bathroom and the constantly dwindling balance in your bankbook.

I don't mean to imply that hiring a general contractor is a panacea. Far from it. There are terrible general contractors out there: some are incompetent, some are corrupt, and some are both. I've seen, and been part of, enough renovation projects to know that even with the best of professionals aboard, problems will crop up. In fact, I'll guarantee that every renovation project, whatever its scope, will either cost more or take longer than originally estimated, if not both. The answer is to take steps to insure the process is as smooth as possible, and to minimize the inevitable cost overruns and/or scheduling delays.

That's where you should be concentrating your efforts, and what this book is about: the overall administration of a renovation project. Rather than trying to take the place of a craftsperson or general contractor, I believe homeowners should instead try to play their administrative role to the best of their abilities. That doesn't mean surrendering control to either a design professional or a general contractor. It means functioning as the chief executive officer of the project: overseeing the planning, making the policy decisions, delegating the authority to implement those decisions, making sure the project stays on course and on time, and paying the bills.

You shouldn't be worrying about whether you need a carbide-tip drill bit, or if the electrician should be called in before the plumber. Instead, you should be concerned with deciding whether renovating is the right solution to your problems; what type of renovation should be done; how much you can afford to spend; who you should call in to get an accurate set of plans or specifications; which general contractor you should select; how you're going to pay for it all; who'll supervise the job; and how you'll resolve potential problems. Subsequent chapters will explain exactly how to do all these things.

The first step is to examine your decision to renovate.

CHAPTER 2

Deciding To Renovate

——

The absence of alternatives clears the mind marvelously.
—HENRY A. KISSINGER

Since you've picked up this book and already made it through chapter 1, it's obvious you're seriously considering renovating your home. You probably already have one or two particular projects in mind, based on your feelings about the house, experience living in it, and current or future life plans. But don't start lining up a general contractor just yet. There is a tremendous amount of preparatory work you must do in order to make this complex process move as smoothly as possible. The first step is to carefully consider whether renovating makes sense financially and emotionally.

When all is said and done it generally makes sense to renovate when you want more space but can't afford to buy another home; want to add character to a generic home; want to boost the value of your home; want to increase the pleasure you get from your home; and/or want to make your home more functional. Let's look at four common situations:

Michael and Barbara Newparent were married in 1980 and moved into Michael's downtown apartment. After five years there, they knew it was time to make a move. Aware of the financial advantages of home ownership, and sick of pouring money down the rental drain, the Newparents decided to become homeowners. They stretched their affordability to the limit, but in the boom market of 1985 all they could manage to buy was a two-bedroom starter house. However, since prices were going up so quickly, the Newparents figured that when it came time for them to start a family they'd be able to sell their house for a profit and use the proceeds to buy a bigger place.

Unfortunately, the real estate market and Barbara's biological clock weren't synchronized. Instead of the value of their house increasing enough for them to be able to afford a new, larger home, it stubbornly remained at what they paid for it in 1985. Now the Newparents can't sell their current home for enough money to buy another home, and don't want to, or perhaps can't, wait any longer to start a family. Their solution is to add space to their current home and turn it into the larger home they'd have bought if they could.

Up the street from the Newparents live their friends Dave Handeman and Tom Oldehouse. Dave and Tom were luckier than the Newparents: They could afford to buy a couple of years earlier and so were able to purchase a four-bedroom house. It needed a great deal of work, however. While nothing was actually falling apart, the inspector told Handeman and Oldehouse they'd need a new roof within three years. The bathroom fixtures were older than either of them, and the kitchen hadn't been updated since the mid-1960s. The plumbing and electrical systems were dated as well. Still, it was all they could afford at the time, and eventually, they told themselves, they'd fix the place up. For the past five years, they've been doing what they could to make the home more livable: removing old wallpaper, painting, stripping paint off the moldings, and installing new kitchen appliances. But the roof has started to leak and the oil burner is about to give up the ghost.

Dave and Tom know they can't afford to buy another home that's the same size but in better shape than theirs. Their solution is to renovate their current home by repairing the roof and updating the electrical, plumbing, and heating systems.

Dave's aunt and uncle are going through much the same sort of dilemma. Fran and Bob Emptynester are part of a generation that didn't look on real estate as an investment. They waited to buy their first home. Remaining renters even after they had their children, the Emptynesters scrimped and saved until they could afford to buy a home big enough for their young family. In 1973 they cashed in their pennies and bought a three bedroom colonial in the suburbs. It was far from a Taj Mahal, but through the years they've taken care of the house, and it has taken care of them—it was a good place to raise children. But their lifestyle has changed a lot in the past eighteen years. Bob's income has increased considerably, and Fran has started her own public relations business. Two years ago they traded in the station wagon for a Mercedes. And since their youngest daughter went to college they've been going out to eat and traveling a lot more.

The Emptynesters would like to trade in their comfortable but characterless colonial for a Georgian with a smaller kitchen and a bigger master bedroom to match their new lifestyle. The problem is they really don't want to move. All their friends are in the old neighborhood and they're rooted in the community—Fran is on the board at the club and Bob is on the parish council. The solution is to renovate their home, remodeling the floor plan to include a master bedroom suite and home office, and turning the characterless family-oriented colonial into the Georgian of their dreams.

The Emptynesters' neighbors, John and Beth Greyhare, can well understand the impact of an empty nest. Their kids have been gone for even longer than the Emptynesters', and are married with kids of their own. The Greyhares always thought they'd move south when John retired, but lately they've been having second thoughts. John's pension and their savings have put them in a better financial position than ever before. And even though their home isn't the ideal spot for a retired couple, they want to stick around to be near the kids and grandchildren. While they thought they'd like a smaller home, after visiting friends who bought a two bedroom apartment, Beth changed her mind.

Still, their current home lacks a lot of the amenities they'd like to have. Beth has wanted a gourmet kitchen for a long time and would love a greenhouse for her flowers. John has always dreamed of a den with a fireplace and skylights. And both of them would love a deck to use for outside entertaining during spring and summer. The solution is to keep their current home, but renovate, turning it into the retirement home of their dreams.

BALANCING FINANCES AND EMOTIONS

These scenarios are but four of the many instances when Americans turn toward home renovation to solve their problems or meet their needs. What all sound renovation decisions have in common is that the needs of the owner or owners have changed and no longer fit their current home, but they're either unwilling or unable to buy a different home. What makes the home renovation decision so complicated, however, is that it involves both financial and emotional elements. In order for the renovation to make sense, it has to balance these sometimes contradictory elements.

Financially, renovations can add to, or detract from, the value of a home. The entire cost of the renovation may be easy to recoup right away, or may never be recoverable. That's because real estate values are based more on location than on the size or quality of the dwelling itself. Homes in a given area often fall into a 30 percent value range. For example: In Michael and Barbara Newparent's neighborhood the biggest, most luxurious home is worth $215,000, and the smallest, sparsest house is worth $185,000. No matter how many additions or changes are made to a home in their area, it will rarely be worth more than 30 percent above the value of the cheapest home.

The difference between homes at the high and low ends of the range can vary. Low-end homes may be like the Newparents' and have only two bedrooms and one bathroom, or may be in poor condition like Dave Handeman and Tom Oldehouse's house. Homes in the middle of the range may be in good condition and have three bedrooms and two bathrooms. Houses in the high end may be in excellent condition and have skylights, fireplaces, fencing, landscaping, and other amenities setting them apart.

In order for a renovation to make financial sense, it should bring a home from one part of the range up to another. If the Newparents add a third bedroom and second bath, and if Handeman and Oldehouse put on a new roof and upgrade their heating, electrical, and plumbing systems, their homes theoretically will increase in value from about $185,000 to $200,000. The older couples, Fran and Bob Emptynester and John and Beth Greyhare, need to be a bit more careful. Assuming their homes are in the middle of the price range, their renovations will make financial sense if the condition of the homes are improved or if popular luxury features and amenities are added. However, if the older couples' homes are already at the high end of the price range, the costs of any changes that are made may never be recouped when the home is sold. For example: If their homes already have three bedrooms and they decide to add a fourth they'll probably never recoup the cost. Similarly, if they add luxury items that none of the other homes in the area have the cost will be sunk money.

Renovation patterns can vary dramatically from one market to another even if they are in close proximity. When my wife and I were first married we lived in the village of Farmingdale, on New York's Long Island. There it seemed as though every homeowner was turning their basement into a den and their garage into another bedroom. When we moved to the village of Woodbury, not more than ten miles away, we found that every homeowner was installing Belgian blocks to line their driveways and slate tiles in their entry halls.

Any improvement to a home that costs more than it adds to a home's value is called a superadequacy—an over-improvement. If, for example, you add a $40,000 central audio/video system to a home, and it adds only $25,000 to the value of the home, it's considered a $15,000 superadequacy. If you spend $50,000 to add a fourth bedroom and third bathroom to a home in an area where all the homes have only three bedrooms and two baths, you may have a $50,000 superadequacy on your hands. According to some studies, more than 20 percent of American homes have been overimproved.

Most real estate experts believe the following improvements add more to the value of a home than they cost: an off-white or neutral color paint job; landscaping and general exterior cosmetics; and moderate kitchen and bathroom upgrades that don't involve unusual colors or deluxe appliances. The same experts say the following improvements generally cost more than they add to the value of a home: swimming pools; hot tubs; outdoor spas; customized or built-in furnishings; expensive woodwork or cabinets; deluxe wall and floor coverings; bidets; tennis courts; and central audio/video systems. Generally, the cost of renovations that improve a home's comfort and convenience, while less dramatic, are more recoverable than the cost of those that increase its size or make it more modern. That's why the experts say, if you've limited dollars it makes sense to invest them in things like the plumbing, electrical, heating, and cooling systems, or the roof, windows, and doors. (For a look at the average costs of various home renovation projects, and the chances of recouping all or part of their costs, see the charts beginning on page 42.)

In addition to affecting value, certain renovations will affect how quickly you'll be able to sell the home. Any cosmetic renovation that reflects neutral or traditional tastes will speed the sale of a home, while anything that reflects unusual personal tastes will slow the sale. Walls that are in good shape and are freshly painted off-white will help sell a home. Wallpaper, no matter how exquisite or expensive, will almost always slow the sale of a home. Homes with white bathroom fixtures sell quicker than homes with colored bathroom fixtures. A deck will almost always speed the sale of a home while a swimming pool will almost always delay it. Elements that aren't traditional or that reflect a particular individual's taste cloud the issue for potential buyers. It's no longer a matter of whether or not they like the home. It becomes a question of how much it will cost to paint over the pink walls, replace the purple bathroom tiles, or fill in the swimming pool.

GETTING PROFESSIONAL ADVICE

The best way to determine how a particular renovation will affect the value and salability of a home is to get an expert opinion. In order to get a handle on the effect a renovation will have on the value of your property, contact a knowledgeable local appraiser. Make sure you choose someone who has extensive residential real estate experience. For a fee of from $150 to $300 they should be able to give you an estimate of how the home's value will be affected by a proposed renovation. They will first research the recent local sales of homes comparable to yours in its current state. Then they will investigate the recent local sales of homes that have the amenities or enhancements you propose to add to your home. They will compare the two sets of selling prices and estimate how much the renovation will add to your home's value.

In order to get an idea of what effect a proposed renovation will have on your home's salability you'll need to contact a real estate broker. Again, it should be someone with extensive residential experience in your particular area. For a fee of from $100 to $200 they should be able to provide you with an educated guess as to whether or not the proposed renovation will speed or delay an eventual sale.

The $250 to $500 you spend on the combined expertise of the appraiser and broker is well worth it. In fact, it's the only way to shed some local factual light on the decision to renovate. Otherwise you'll be basing your decision on emotions and national averages.

After obtaining this advice it's time to move out of the realm of finances and into the land of emotions. If you're a purely pragmatic individual, you'll never do anything that doesn't add to the value of a home, doesn't improve its salability, or that won't enable you to recoup its cost. But that's not how most of us live our lives, nor should it be. A home is more than a financial investment. It's where you eat, sleep, work, make love, fight, laugh, cry, play, relax, raise your children, celebrate your holidays, and mourn your losses. While its financial importance cannot be over-estimated, neither can its emotional power. A home can be a refuge, a safe haven, a protective umbrella from the storms of the outside world for ourselves and our family. And the more wonderful you make your home, the more comforting and rewarding your life becomes. Having a magnificent home won't turn your life around, but it will make you happier.

After calculating the financial return on a proposed renovation, and its effect on the home's salability, you must factor into the equation the emotional or psycholog-ical benefits it offers. The Greyhares may never be able to fully recoup the cost of adding a greenhouse to their home. It potentially could make it a little bit more difficult to sell. But how will it affect their lives? How much pleasure will it bring them? If the answers are that it will improve their lives and bring them a great deal of pleasure, then the money that's not recouped isn't sunk—it has been invested in themselves and their lives.

I had an in-ground swimming pool built at my farm in Connecticut. Swimming pools are probably the ultimate in sunk investments—pardon the pun. Their sizable cost is rarely recoverable and they invariably complicate the sale of a home. Knowing all that I still chose to have it built. (Even worse, I also converted a chicken coop into a pool house.) You see, I don't look on the farm as just a financial investment. It has become the focus for my extended family. On holidays and on summer weekends my parents, my children, and my grandchildren come to the farm. As my children grow older and start their own families, all of our lives become increasingly separate. The farm serves as an anchor, a foundation, a place where we can all come together and be a family once more. And the pool is there to increase our pleasure. On weekends in the summer we can all cool off at the pool—and be together. It's not that the pool brings the kids "home," it's that it makes it more comfortable once they're home. To me, that's well worth the money I've "sunk" in the pool.

In effect, the question you must ask yourself is whether or not a potentially nonrecoverable renovation will bring enough pleasure to your life to justify the cost. The answer usually depends on how long you intend to remain in this particular home. Think in terms of five-year increments. Can you envision selling this home within five years, within ten, within fifteen? If you were to sell within five years, would the emotional and psychological benefits from a renovation still outweigh its nonrecoverable cost? How about if you sold in ten years? The shorter the length of time you see yourself remaining in a home, the more you should stress the financial elements of a renovation. The magic line where financial and psychological elements start to come into balance is generally around ten years. The diagram below illustrates the principle.

If you can see yourself getting ten years worth of pleasure out of a $9,000 greenhouse, you might want to go ahead with the renovation. But if you could see yourself moving in ten years you probably wouldn't want to put $20,000 into a swimming pool. Once you break the ten-year mark the emotional element of a renovation starts to outweigh the financial—that's when renovations such as adding a swimming pool may become feasible.

There's a hidden trap to factoring emotions into the decision-making process. We all have a tendency to justify and rationalize in order to get what we want. I've had clients dramatically overimprove their homes, pouring more money than was prudent into a renovation. When I warned them of the dangers, and pointed out that they'd never be able to recoup any of this money, they brushed me off. "We're never going to sell this home," they said.

BALANCING FINANCIAL AND EMOTIONAL ISSUES

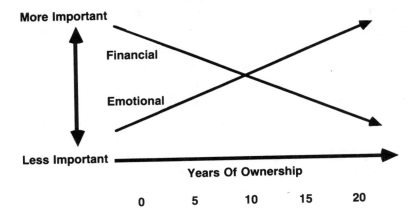

"We'll be in it forever. We're turning it into the home of our dreams." Almost invariably, however, they ended up selling the home of their dreams, usually within ten years.

At the age of forty you may see yourself as being eternally happy in a dazzling contemporary home, secluded on two wooded acres. The idea of driving fifteen minutes for a gallon of milk doesn't bother you. By the time you turn fifty you may be fed up with living in a glass bubble in the middle of nowhere and long for a warmer, more relaxed home, closer to, or even in, town. I'm not saying you shouldn't trust your instincts, but temper those gut feelings with a bit of pragmatism. Remember: Your dreams will change.

The exceptions that prove the rule are people with more than one home. Generally they do hold on to at least one of their homes—generally whichever is more traditional—for their entire lives. I believe the reason is that having two homes allows them to indulge their changing dreams. One home represents the solidity and permanence of their lives, the other their changing tastes. That's why you'll almost always find people with two homes decorating them in extremely different styles. For instance, my Connecticut farmhouse is rather formal and is furnished with antiques, while my Martha's Vineyard beach house is very informal and eclectic.

Once you've decided that renovation makes sense in your circumstances, the next step is to think about what type of renovation best suits your needs. Home renovations generally fall into one of five categories: cosmetic face-lifts, system upgrades, space additions, luxury additions, or remodeling. No one knows better than you which type of renovation will bring you the most pleasure and satisfaction or is the most essential. But remember, this isn't solely an emotional decision—there are financial elements to it as well which should be considered.

COSMETIC FACE-LIFTS

Cosmetic face-lifts are projects that improve the appearance of the home, such as painting the exterior or interior; landscaping the yard and grounds; replacing or refinishing the floors; replacing appliances; replacing, refacing, or restoring cabinets; and replacing or refinishing bathroom fixtures. Most face-lifts are generally inexpensive when compared to other types of renovations. They offer the most immediate, but least lasting, return on investment. And in many cases they're the simplest projects requiring the least time or disruption of the household. That doesn't mean there may not be surprises lurking.

For example, let's say you want to redo the kitchen. A face-lift might involve buying new appliances and light fixtures and having them installed; refinishing or refacing the cabinets; repainting the walls and ceiling; and having a new floor surface installed. The cost of such a project could be almost entirely recouped, especially if you already have a good floor plan, and stick with neutral colors and midrange appliances. It would cost considerably less than gutting the kitchen and starting from scratch with a new floor plan and new cabinets. And it shouldn't take an unreasonable amount of time, if the trades are properly coordinated. However, over time the value it adds to the home will decrease as the appliances age and become outmoded, and the finishes lose their sparkle and show signs of wear. In addition, if there are any underlying problems not initially visible—such as a leak behind the sink or dishwasher—the job could grow more complex, costly, and time-consuming.

SYSTEM UPGRADES

System upgrades are renovations that improve the functional quality of a home such as replacing or improving the electrical, plumbing, heating and/or cooling systems; replacing windows and doors; repairing or replacing the roof; or completely insulating and weatherstripping the entire home. System upgrades aren't very glamorous and won't offer much emotional return on your investment. However, they can add immeasurably to your comfort and happiness in subtle ways. They offer a good return on investment, especially in the short term, but can be complex and costly.

Let's look at the upgrading of a plumbing system as an example. You're not going to beam with pride and point out the new pipes and hot-water heater to all your friends when they visit. But having enough hot water so you, your spouse, and your children can all take showers in the morning and still get to work and school on time, can add a great deal to your pleasure in life. The job could be as simple as replacing the hot-water heater and a couple of shower heads and faucets. However, it might also require getting behind the walls and replacing pipes throughout the house—a sizable and expensive undertaking. The cost of upgrading a system will be recouped in an increased resale price as long as the system is young. As time goes on and it ages—and shows its age—you'll be less likely to make the money back. Still, inadequate systems can make your life miserable and will also certainly turn off all but the most optimistic potential purchasers. And, if the system upgrade has reduced energy costs, it may already have paid for itself when it comes time to sell.

SPACE ADDITIONS

Space additions are projects that add to the actual living space of a home such as: finishing a basement; finishing or expanding an attic; expanding dormers into additional rooms; converting a garage into living space; or building an extension on the home. It's tough to generalize about space additions because there are so many variables. They can be very costly or affordable, simple or complex, valuable or nearly worthless. That's why it pays to be very thoughtful and deliberate when contemplating a space addition.

As I wrote earlier in this chapter, if by adding space you bring your home up to the norm for the area, it can be an excellent investment offering a sizable and long-term return. However, if you add more space than most of the homes in the area the money could be sunk. As a rule, aboveground space additions are a better investment than below-ground additions, since no matter what you do, a basement is still a basement. It may superficially look like a bedroom, bathroom, and laundry room, but it won't fool anyone. It will be dark, damp, cold, and have low ceilings. Still, if all the other homes in the area have finished basements, or if you're desperate for more space, it may make sense. Aboveground additions can also be a poor investment, perhaps even detracting from the home's value. If you expand an attic or add a wing, and in the process, destroy the external appearance and character of a home, you'll end up lowering its value. However, a well-done addition, which fits or even augments a home's appearance, and which reflects the needs and wants of most buyers, can add substantially to both the home's value and your enjoyment of life.

LUXURY ADDITIONS

Luxury additions involve incorporating an amenity into the home that adds to the comfort or pleasure of the occupants, such as adding fireplaces; darkrooms; workshops; skylights; swimming pools; tennis courts; central air conditioning; central vacuuming; security systems; greenhouses; decks; hot tubs; and/or central audio/video systems. The actual labor involved in installing these luxury items isn't as important as the quality of the item itself. As long as it's installed properly, the amount of pleasure you get from a hot tub, for example, will depend on whether or not you select a high-quality product. And since most of these products are designed to be retrofitted—added to an existing structure—the installation shouldn't be too complex or costly.

This is the one type of renovation where you usually must come down on one side or the other—sound investment or emotional enjoyment. With a couple of notable (and perhaps temporary) exceptions—fireplaces and skylights—you may not be able to recoup the money you put into adding an amenity to a home. That's because they almost all represent a unique personal choice or a trend. If you're an avid photographer, converting a walk-in closet or extra bathroom into a darkroom can be wonderful. However, unless you end up selling the home to another photographer, it will probably be sunk money. In fact, it could be a negative factor. Nonphotographers will see the darkroom, guess how much it will cost to turn it back into a closet or bathroom, and reduce their offer by that amount. Still, if you intend to live in the home for an extended period of time, and are dying for a darkroom, consider the money spent as an investment in mental health and happiness.

Be aware that what's trendy today may not be tomorrow. Today, for instance, some of the popular amenities are: restaurant-quality kitchen appliances; adding a pond, rather than a pool; granite rather than marble in a bathroom; and stone walls rather than wooden fencing outside. In ten years, however, having these amenities could make your home look dated. Before you do anything trendy, think of how you would react today to a kitchen or dining room done entirely in knotty pine, and remember that was once trendy too.

REMODELING

Remodeling involves anything that alters the floor plan of a home and can include anything from redoing a kitchen or bathroom entirely, to combining two bedrooms and a bathroom into a master bedroom suite with a dressing room and two bathrooms. While it's tough to generalize about remodeling projects, they're usually expensive, complex, and costly. They can be a great investment if they add something to a home that other homes in the area have—a well designed, eat-in kitchen, for instance. However, they could also destroy the flow or character of a home, dramatically reducing its value.

It's even possible for a remodeling project to become blatantly absurd. Since new construction is less costly than rebuilding, there comes a point where it would make more sense simply to knock the whole house down and start over again. I've seen people who have just bought a home commission such absurd remodeling jobs. Many times, the professionals involved in such foolhardy projects won't even suggest total reconstruction. They're afraid it will lose them the job. Even if the pros do point out the foolishness of the project to the homeowners, often they can't accept it. They feel they've bought this house and they must have something to show for it. So, in effect, they preserve a chimney and fireplace and build an entirely new home all around it.

I was involved in one such job. I represented an extremely wealthy gentleman who decided he wanted to add a home in Connecticut to his list of residences. With the help of an excellent real estate broker I discovered a lovely home for him. He agreed with my selection and we quickly closed the deal. But since money was no object he decided to renovate the home to suit his needs and tastes. He fell under the spell of a young architect whose love of exotic materials—and sizable fees—turned the renovation into a circus. The project became more and more absurd as costs escalated out of all proportion. The general contractor, who I respected enormously, remained silent. Later he verified my suspicion that it would have cost less money to knock down the original home and build a new one from scratch. When I asked him why he didn't tell that to the owner, he retorted with his own question. "How would you react," he asked, "if I told you to knock down a home you had just purchased for $500,000?" He then answered his own question. "You would fire me from the job and hire someone else who would be happy to do the job with no questions asked. At least I will make every effort to control costs and keep the owner aware of the escalating price tag."

A good remodeling job will be invisible; people should be able to walk through the home and not realize it has been remodeled. That's not as easy as it sounds. Converting the kitchen and dining room of a small Victorian home into a large, open-plan, great room, may be just what your family needs and wants. However, it almost certainly will change the feeling of the home; after all, Victorians don't have great rooms. The secret to recouping an investment in remodeling is to make sure the new floor plan doesn't reflect a unique need or desire. You may want a kitchenette on the second floor, but most people will be taken aback by it.

As with the general decision to renovate, the selection of a type of renovation requires you to balance the financial and emotional aspects of home ownership. It's not easy, but it's better to open your eyes to the process before you must open your wallet. Assuming you now have a good idea what type of renovation makes the most sense financially and emotionally, it's time to figure out if you can afford to pay for it.

PROJECT ANALYSIS CHARTS

The following charts will help you get a better idea of exactly how much various home renovation projects will cost and how likely this cost is to be recouped.

Much of the information comes from the R.S. Means Company, of Kingston, Massachusetts, the world's leading experts on construction costs and the primary source of pricing guides for contractors. The company has just published its first consumer-oriented pricing guides, appropriately titled *Home Improvement Costs for Interior Projects* and *Home Improvement Costs for Exterior Projects*. In addition to prices for various projects, the books contain breakdowns for parts and labor; approximations of how long the projects will theoretically take in man hours for professionals, handymen, and amateurs; and notes on things the person or persons doing the work should watch out for. I heartily recommend them for those who wish to immerse themselves in the world of renovation.

The chart beginning on page 42 is an analysis of the price and return on investment potential for a variety of home renovation projects. The first column contains a description of the project. Remember: Of necessity these represent very generalized projects. Every actual renovation project, from the installation of an attic fan to the addition of a family room, is a custom job based on your individual taste and the peculiarities of your home. Accordingly, the price information in column two should only be seen as an estimate. These numbers are national averages that will be tailored specifically to your location by using the second chart. Bear in mind: These price estimates are for contractor's fees and include materials.

The third column contains my best determination for the odds of your recouping all or most of the cost of a renovation. These judgments are based on discussions with appraisers from around the country and on interviews with the editors of leading home improvement magazines who conduct their own annual surveys of return on investment. These judgments are best case scenarios that assume the projects are designed and executed flawlessly. The fourth column contains comments.

The chart beginning on page 57 is a listing of Means's location multipliers. These numbers can be used to take the general pricing estimates from the first chart and turn them into specific estimates for your area. Scan down the first column for your state, and then the second column for the first three numbers of your zip code. Take the number listed in the third column and multiply it by the national price estimate from the first chart to determine a regional price estimate.

COST AND RETURN POTENTIAL

Project Description	Estimated Cost	Return Potential				Comments
		Exc	Good	Fair	Poor	
Ventilate attic	$555	√				projects that maintain the soundness of the structure will be indirectly reflected in the eventual selling price.
Finish breezeway	$6,173 (w/screens) $9,316 (w/windows)		√			must be done in keeping with the style of the structure and not appear to be an afterthought or compromise.
New breezeway (10' × 16')	$11,583	√				must be done in keeping with the style of the structure and not appear to be an afterthought or compromise.
Carport: single, attached (11' × 21')	$2,384			√		must be done in keeping with the style of the structure and not appear to be an afterthought or compromise.

Project Description	Estimated Cost	Return Potential				Comments
		Exc	Good	Fair	Poor	
Carport: double freestanding (20' × 21')	$6,988		√			must be done in keeping with the style of the structure and not appear to be an afterthought or compromise.
Deck: ground level (8' × 10')	$1,541			√		price does not include painting, staining, or finishing.
Deck: elevated (10' × 16')	$2,990		√			if more than 4' above grade, or situated over sloping terrain, it will cost more. Price does not include painting, staining, or finishing.
Deck: elevated Redwood (12' × 12')	$6,230		√			if more than 4' above grade, or situated over sloping terrain, it will cost more.
Deck: elevated "L" shape (8'×16', 8'×12')	$4,591		√			if more than 4' above grade, or situated over sloping terrain, it will cost more. Price does not include painting, staining, or finishing.

Project Description	Estimated Cost	Return Potential				Comments
		Exc	Good	Fair	Poor	
Deck: roof (8′ × 16′)	$3,149		√			price does not include painting, staining, or finishing.
Dormer	$2,344 (4′ gable) $4,592 (7′ gable) $4,291 (12′ shed) $5,966 (20′ shed) $7,293 (30′ shed)	√				price does not include interior finishing.
Main entry door: insulated steel	$1,000		√			prominent features on a facade must be in character with the rest of the home.
Patio doors: French-style	$3,088		√			
Patio doors: sliding glass	$1,603			√		
Basement doors: bulkhead	$3,151			√		
Additional window	$772 (3′ × 4′) $2,962 (bay-style)		√			must be done in keeping with the style of the structure and not appear to be an afterthought or compromise.

Project Description	Estimated Cost	Return Potential				Comments
		Exc	Good	Fair	Poor	
Garage: single, attached (12' × 22')	$8,783		√			must be done in keeping with the style of the structure and not appear to be an afterthought or compromise.
Garage: double freestanding (22' × 22')	$11,357	√				price does not include the cost of adding electrical service. must be done in keeping with the style of the structure and not appear to be an afterthought or compromise.
Octagonal gazebo	$3,791 (4' sides) $9,669 (6' sides)				√	
Lean-to green-house	$9,376 (5'6" × 10'6") $17,742 (8' × 16')				√	
Insulated sun room	$11,063 (5'6" × 10'6") $23,548 (10'6" × 18')	√				
Wheelchair ramp (4' × 15')	$2,154				√	
Garden pond (12' × 16')	$3,791				√	

Project Description	Estimated Cost	Return Potential				Comments
		Exc	Good	Fair	Poor	
Retaining wall (wood, 2' high, 20' long)	$1,742			√		
Fencing (wooden board, 4' high, 320' long)	$6,207		√			must be both functional and in keeping with the character of the home.
Outdoor post light and outlet	$506	√				
Walkway: brick in sand (3' wide, 30' long)	$978			√		
Residing: wood clapboards (16'4" × 135')	$11,064	√				
Exterior painting (primer and two coats on 2,000 square feet)	$2,764	√				
Patio: brick in sand (6' × 12')	$1,287			√		
Patio: brick in mortar (12' × 12')	$1,941			√		
Patio: concrete	$312 (6' × 12') $1,043 (12' × 16')				√	
Patio: flagstone (12' × 12')	$3,186			√		

Project Description	Estimated Cost	Return Potential				Comments
		Exc	Good	Fair	Poor	
Enclose porch	$3,325 (8' × 14' w/screens) $6,437 (12' × 16' w/sliding glass doors)			√		
Enclose and insulate porch (6' × 12' w/windows)	$3,921	√				must fit the character and floor plan of the home.
Entryway steps: wooden	$900		√			prominent features on a facade must be in character with the rest of the home.
Wooden play structure	$3,784				√	
Redwood hot tub (6' diameter tub in 12' × 14' deck)	$5,824				√	
Reroofing (removal of old roofing and replacement with 1,000 square feet of asphalt shingles)	$1,706		√			projects that maintain the soundness of the structure will be indirectly reflected in the eventual selling price.

Project Description	Estimated Cost	Return Potential				Comments
		Exc	Good	Fair	Poor	
Ground floor room addition	$6,966 (8' × 8') $7,687 (8' × 12') $13,645 (12' × 16') $34,103 (20' × 24')	√				must fit the character and floor plan of the home.
Second-story room addition	$8,576 (8' × 12') $25,007 (20' × 24')	√				must fit the character and floor plan of the home.
Security upgrade (upgraded door and window locks, door viewers, flood-lighting)	$1,833			√		
Utility shed (10' × 12')	$5,591				√	
Garbage and re-cycling shed (2'10" × 5')	$1,490				√	

Project Description	Estimated Cost	Return Potential				Comments
		Exc	Good	Fair	Poor	
Skylight	$817 (fixed 24" × 24" bubble) $1,717 (ventilating 52" × 52" bubble) $1,343 (fixed 24" × 48" sky window) $1,733 (operable 48" × 52" sky window)	√				
Finish attic	$5,889 (half finished: 16' × 20') $14,558 (fully finished: 16' × 36')	√				
Whole-house fan	$845	√				cost will be recouped in lower utility bills.
Finish basement: below grade (24' × 20')	$7,709				√	
Finish basement: walk-out (24' × 40')	$16,217	√				shouldn't result in the elimination of all storage space.

Project Description	Estimated Cost	Return Potential				Comments
		Exc	Good	Fair	Poor	
Standard half-bathroom (4′ × 6′ w/toilet and sink)	$2,312	√				neutral colors and styles will increase the return.
Deluxe half-bathroom (4′ × 6′ w/toilet and sink)	$3,212				√	the more idiosyncratic a renovation, the less likely its cost will be recouped.
Standard full bathroom (7′ × 8′ w/toilet, sink, tub/shower)	$4,499	√				neutral colors and styles will increase the return.
Deluxe full bathroom (7′ × 8′ w/toilet, sink, tub/shower)	$6,633				√	the more idiosyncratic a renovation, the less likely its cost will be recouped.
Standard master bathroom (8′ × 10′ w/toilet, twin sinks, tub, and shower)	$7,023	√				neutral colors and styles will increase the return.
Deluxe master bathroom (8′ × 10′ w/toilet, twin sinks, tub, and shower)	$10,788				√	the more idiosyncratic a renovation, the less likely its cost will be recouped.

Project Description	Estimated Cost	Return Potential				Comments
		Exc	Good	Fair	Poor	
Deluxe bath/spa (12′ × 18′ w/toilet, bidet, twin sinks, whirlpool tub, large shower)	$21,316				√	the more idiosyncratic a renovation, the less likely its cost will be recouped.
Sauna (6′ × 6′)	$8,661				√	
Tile bathroom walls (7′ × 8′)	$1,041			√		
Ventilate bathroom	$587			√		
Replace vanity and lavatory	$1,178			√		
Replace toilet	$445			√		
Standard closet (48″ × 30″)	$1,910	√				best if added to a bedroom which has none.
Closet under stairs (3′ × 12′)	$600			√		
Walk-in cedar closet in attic (6′ × 8′)	$1,789				√	
Linen closet (18″ × 30″)	$861	√				best if added to a home that has none.
Laundry center (3′ × 6′)	$1,001	√				best if added to a home that has none.
Pantry cabinet (24″ × 24″ × 84″)	$1,043			√		

Project Description	Estimated Cost	Return Potential				Comments
		Exc	Good	Fair	Poor	
Attic kneewall storage unit (28″ × 30″)	$487			√		
Replace interior door	$266			√		
Wainscoting and chair rail (12′ × 15′)	$1,768		√			
Upgrade electrical system (increase service to 200 AMP, add new panel board, modernize some receptacles and fixtures)	$2,225	√				maintenance and improvement of systems will result in a higher selling price.
Fireplace: freestanding (5′ × 5′ × 13′)	$3,263			√		
Fireplace: built-in (5′ × 6′ × 13′)	$3,796		√			
Fireplace: masonry (6′ × 6′ × 20′)	$4,663	√				adding a first is a much better investment than adding a second or third.
Flooring: oak strip (12′ × 16′)	$1,718	√				
Flooring: parquet (12′ × 14′)	$1,155		√			

Project Description	Estimated Cost	Return Potential				Comments
		Exc	Good	Fair	Poor	
Flooring: vinyl sheet (11′ × 11′6″)	$1,295			√		
Flooring: ceramic tile (8′ × 12′)	$970	√				neutral colors and styles will increase the return.
Garage conversion (22′ × 22′)	$11,503			√		must be coupled with the creation of another form of vehicle protection; i.e., adding a carport.
Insulation (6,000 square feet)	$1,397	√				cost will be recouped in lower utility bills.
Standard wall kitchen (6′6″ × 14′)	$6,358	√				neutral colors and styles will increase the return.
Deluxe wall kitchen (6′6″ × 14′)	$12,215				√	the more idiosyncratic a renovation, the less likely its cost will be recouped.
Standard corridor kitchen (11′ × 11′6″)	$9,004	√				neutral colors and styles will increase the return.
Deluxe corridor kitchen (11′ × 11′6″)	$14,187				√	the more idiosyncratic a renovation, the less likely its cost will be recouped.

Project Description	Estimated Cost	Return Potential				Comments
		Exc	Good	Fair	Poor	
Standard L-kitchen (8' × 12')	$7,608	√				neutral colors and styles will increase the return.
Deluxe L-kitchen (8' × 12')	$11,471				√	the more idiosyncratic a renovation, the less likely its cost will be recouped.
Standard U-kitchen (9'6" × 10'6")	$9,084	√				neutral colors and styles will increase the return.
Deluxe U-kitchen (9'6" × 10'6")	$13,623				√	the more idiosyncratic a renovation, the less likely its cost will be recouped.
Standard peninsula kitchen (9'6" × 13')	$12,416	√				neutral colors and styles will increase the return.
Deluxe peninsula kitchen (9'6" × 10'6")	$18,420				√	the more idiosyncratic a renovation, the less likely its cost will be recouped.
Standard island kitchen (11'6" × 14'6")	$12,258	√				neutral colors and styles will increase the return.

LOCATION MULTIPLIERS*

State	United States Zip Code	Multiplier	State	United States Zip Code	Multiplier
AL	350–355	0.82		952–953	1.14
	356–358	0.83		954	1.13
	359–364	0.82		955–961	1.10
	365–366	0.91	CO	800–804	0.96
	367–369	0.82		805–807	0.98
AK	995–999	1.24		808–814	0.92
AZ	850–857	0.93		815–816	0.97
	859–865	0.94	CT	060–062	0.96
AR	716–717	0.83		063	0.98
	718	0.82		064–065	0.96
	719–722	0.83		066–067	0.95
	723–724	0.87		068–069	1.00
	725–726	0.83	DE	197–199	1.00
	727–729	0.84	DC	200–205	0.94
CA	900–918	1.13	FL	320–322	0.85
	920–921	1.11		323–324	0.78
	922–925	1.13		325	0.82
	926–927	1.15		326	0.87
	928	1.14		327–328	0.86
	930	1.15		329–333	0.85
	931	1.16		334	0.90
	932–933	1.10		335–338	0.86
	934	1.17		339	0.88
	935	1.09	GA	300–303	0.84
	936–937	1.12		304	0.83
	939	1.09		305–306	0.84
	940–948	1.21		307	0.86
	949	1.22		308–309	0.87
	950–951	1.26		310–312	0.83

* To determine a regional price estimate, multiply the number in column three by the national price estimate from the chart beginning on page 42.

State	United States Zip Code	Multiplier	State	United States Zip Code	Multiplier
	313–314	0.84		473	0.95
	315	0.81		474	1.00
	316	0.80		475–478	0.96
	317	0.79		479	0.97
	318–319	0.80	IA	500–503	0.93
HI	967–968	1.22		504–507	0.91
ID	832–834	0.94		508	0.94
	835	1.07		510–511	0.89
	836–837	0.93		512–513	0.85
	838	1.07		514	0.94
IL	600–606	1.05		515–516	0.93
	609	1.04		520	0.96
	610–611	1.00		521	0.95
	612	1.01		522–525	0.94
	613–614	1.00		526	0.97
	615–616	0.99		527–528	0.93
	617	0.97	KS	660–662	0.99
	618–619	0.98		664–666	0.87
	620–622	1.02		667	0.89
	623	0.95		668	0.87
	624	0.98		669	0.91
	625–627	0.96		670–673	0.88
	628–629	1.02		674–677	0.89
IN	460–462	0.99		678–679	0.88
	463–464	1.04	KY	400–402	0.91
	465–466	0.97		403–405	0.88
	467–468	0.95		406–409	0.91
	469	0.96		410	0.98
	470	0.98		411–412	0.97
	471	0.92		413–414	0.89
	472	1.00		415–416	0.97

State	United States Zip Code	Multiplier	State	United States Zip Code	Multiplier
	417–418	0.89	MI	480–482	1.09
	420	1.01		484–485	0.99
	421–422	0.93		486–487	0.91
	423–424	0.98		488–489	0.98
	425–426	0.89		490–491	0.95
	427	0.92		492	0.98
LA	700–701	0.87		493–496	0.90
	703–704	0.86		497	0.91
	705	0.88		498–499	0.95
	706–708	0.86	MN	550–551	1.02
	710–714	0.81		553–554	1.03
ME	039–042	0.87		556–558	0.93
	043–048	0.88		559	0.95
	049	0.89		560	1.01
MD	206	0.98		561–562	0.93
	207–208	0.96		563	1.00
	209–212	0.98		564	1.01
	214–216	0.97		565–567	0.81
	217	1.00	MS	386–387	0.84
	218–219	0.97		388	0.79
MA	010–011	1.03		389–392	0.84
	012	0.99		393	0.81
	013	1.01		394–395	0.85
	014–016	1.09		396	0.82
	017	1.17		397	0.79
	018	1.06	MO	630–633	0.99
	019	1.18		634	1.09
	020–022	1.17		635	0.85
	023–025	1.02		636–637	0.99
	026	1.03		638–639	1.14
	027	1.02		640–641	1.00

State	United States Zip Code	Multiplier	State	United States Zip Code	Multiplier
	644–646	0.85		084	1.08
	647	0.99		085–089	1.07
	648	0.85	NM	870–878	0.88
	650–652	1.09		879–880	0.79
	653	1.04		881–884	0.90
	654–655	1.09	NY	100–104	1.31
	656–658	0.85		105–109	1.24
MT	590–599	0.92		110–119	1.31
NE	680–681	0.88		120–122	0.97
	683–685	0.86		123	0.98
	686	0.82		124–127	1.26
	687	0.88		128–129	1.00
	688–691	0.85		130–132	0.99
	692	0.84		133–136	0.89
	693	0.90		137–139	0.90
NV	890–891	1.03		140–143	1.08
	893	1.01		144–146	1.00
	894–898	0.99		147	1.08
NH	030–034	0.88		148–149	0.92
	035	0.86	NC	270	0.77
	036–037	0.84		271	0.79
	038	0.90		272–274	0.77
NJ	070–072	1.13		275–276	0.79
	073	1.09		277	0.77
	074–076	1.08		278	0.79
	077	1.07		279	0.82
	078	1.10		280–282	0.78
	079	1.13		283	0.79
	080	1.09		284	0.77
	081–082	1.08		285	0.80
	083	1.09		286	0.78

State	United States Zip Code	Multiplier	State	United States Zip Code	Multiplier
	287–288	0.77	PA	150–154	1.02
	289	0.78		155	1.07
ND	580–584	0.82		156	1.02
	585–588	0.83		157–159	1.07
OH	430–432	1.00		160–162	1.03
	433	0.97		163	0.95
	434–436	1.00		164–165	0.96
	437–438	0.99		166	1.09
	439	0.95		167	1.01
	440–441	1.13		168	0.96
	442–443	1.00		169	0.98
	444–445	0.98		170–172	0.97
	446–447	0.95		173–176	0.98
	448–452	1.01		177–178	1.00
	453–454	0.98		179	0.97
	455	0.96		180–183	1.05
	456	1.01		184–188	0.96
	457	0.99		189	0.98
	458	1.00		190–194	1.12
OK	730–731	0.85		195–196	0.96
	734–735	0.86	RI	028–029	0.97
	736	0.85	SC	290–293	0.76
	737–739	0.88		294–295	0.77
	740–744	0.89		296–298	0.76
	745	0.85		299	0.77
	746	0.88	SD	570–575	0.86
	747–749	0.85		576	0.87
OR	970–972	1.02		577	0.88
	973	1.01	TN	370–372	0.84
	974–977	1.00		373–374	0.86
	978–979	0.94		376	0.84

State	United States Zip Code	Multiplier	State	United States Zip Code	Multiplier
	377–379	0.83		798–799	0.79
	380–381	0.87	UT	840–846	0.90
	382	0.84	VT	050–059	0.86
	383	0.79	VA	220–228	0.94
	384–385	0.84		229–232	0.87
TX	750	0.93		233–235	0.82
	751	0.86		236	0.83
	752–753	0.90		237	0.82
	754–756	0.92		238–239	0.87
	757	0.93		240–241	0.82
	758–759	0.82		242	0.86
	760–761	0.88		243	0.82
	762	0.95		244	0.87
	763	0.85		245	0.85
	764	0.88		246	0.81
	765–768	0.83	WA	980–981	0.97
	769	0.86		982	0.96
	770–772	0.89		983–985	1.03
	773	0.86		986	1.06
	774–775	0.89		988	0.97
	776–777	0.91		989	1.03
	778	0.85		990–994	1.00
	779	0.82	WV	247–253	0.98
	780–784	0.83		254	0.97
	785	0.84		255–257	0.96
	786–787	0.83		258–259	0.98
	788	0.84		260–261	0.96
	789	0.87		262–265	1.01
	790–791	0.84		266–267	0.98
	792	0.81		268	1.01
	793–797	0.82	WI	530–532	0.99

State	United States Zip Code	Multiplier
	534	1.00
	535–539	0.94
	540	1.08
	541–543	0.95
	544–545	0.96
	546	0.95
	547–548	1.00
	549	0.95
WY	820	0.91
	821	0.89
	822–823	0.91
	824	0.89
	825–827	0.90
	828	0.89
	829–831	0.91

Province	City	Multiplier
NB	Saint John	0.96
	Moncton	0.96
NF	St. John's	0.97
NS	Halifax	0.96
ON	Hamilton	1.16
	London	1.12
	Ottawa	1.13
	Sudbury	1.12
	Toronto	1.18
PE	Charlotte-town	1.00
PQ	Montreal	1.10
	Quebec	1.12
	Regina	1.08
SK	Saskatoon	1.08

Canada (reflect Canadian currency)		
Province	City	Multiplier
AB	Calgary	1.04
	Edmonton	1.05
BC	Vancouver	1.08
MB	Winnipeg	1.04

CHAPTER 3

Calculating Affordability

—

*The average family exists only on paper
and its average budget is a fiction,
invented by statisticians for the
convenience of statisticians. . . . There
is no sense in attempting to fit into a
ready-to-wear financial pattern which
ignores your own personal wants and
desires.*

—Sylvia Porter

There's no set rule about how much you can afford to spend on home renovation. And even if there was some formula or guideline I'd advise you to ignore it. Rules of affordability are generally set by those doing the lending, such as banks, who are concerned you'll stretch too far and be unable to pay. It's easy to understand their eagerness to make affordability decisions for you, and the willingness of most homeowners to accept these outside judgments.

Lenders are only concerned with being paid back. Therefore, it's in their interest for you to be very conservative in your borrowing. They don't look at your willingness to make sacrifices, to scrimp, save, and cut back on other things, in order to turn your house into the home of your dreams. For them it's strictly a matter of comparing your income to your debt. Homeowners all too often fall into the trap of letting a banker, for instance, calculate their affordability. They sit down with a loan officer, present proof of their income and evidence of their debts, ask the banker how much she'll lend them, and believe that her assessment is an accurate measure of their affordability. Relying on an outside judgment is certainly easy. And it pretty much guarantees you'll have no trouble actually getting approved for the loan. But I think it's foolish.

No third party can fully grasp how important this renovation project is to you and your family. No one else can understand what it will mean for you to have the kitchen you've always wanted, a fireplace in your living room, or a deck adjacent to your dining room. You're the only person who can decide how much these amenities or additions are worth, and how much you're willing to sacrifice to get them if you don't simply have a bundle of cash sitting around. Sure, this places a burden on you. You'll need to do some serious calculations and make some hard decisions. You'll need to examine your lifestyle objectively, perhaps for the first time since you bought the home. And you'll probably need to sell your personal estimate of affordability to others. But remember: It's your home and it's the quality of your life.

You've made the choice to invest time, energy, and money into it, with the intent of extending your ownership for a longer period of time than anticipated. Relying on someone else to make the affordability judgment for you isn't an expediency, it's surrendering control. The decision to renovate is a proactive one. You're taking charge of your life, renovating it as well as your home. So sharpen some pencils, grab a legal pad, put new batteries in your calculator, and roll up your sleeves: You're about to examine your life.

STEP #1: WHERE DOES ALL YOUR MONEY GO?

Most of us have no idea where our money goes. We deposit our paychecks, pay our bills, and if money is left over we either buy things with it, or save it, depending on our personalities. And these savings, if you in fact have any, are probably targeted at some specific future responsibility—a vacation, retirement, or perhaps your child's college education. Unless forced to, we almost never take a full accounting of our spending habits. Every spring we dump a shoe box full of receipts onto the desk of our accountant, or worse our own kitchen table, and try to make enough sense of the mess to fill out our tax returns. When a bank requests information for a loan, we scramble to come up with the numbers and documentation they need. But in order to get a true gauge on affordability you'll need to put an end to this unthinking use of money. From this day on—or at least until you've lined up your financing—you're going to keep track of every penny you spend. Before you can start this new policy of fiscal responsibility, however, you must figure out where your money went in the past.

The judgment of how much you can spend on a renovation will be based first on a monthly figure, not a single lump sum. That's because most of us just don't have enough surplus cash sitting around to pay for a major renovation. Instead, you're going to need to borrow the money from a bank, a credit union, or perhaps a relative. Regardless of who does the lending, you're going to be paying it back monthly, not in a single large payment sometime off in the distant future. The idea is to determine how much you can afford to pay back each month, and use that figure to calculate your affordability.

Even if your renovation project is a small one, your estimate of affordability should be evaluated on a monthly basis. While it makes sense to pay cash for projects costing less than $3,000 to avoid the interest and finance charges, you'll probably still need to find the money in your budget. I believe everyone's first financial goal should be to establish an emergency cash reserve large enough to sustain themselves and their family for from four to six months. If you've already done that, have an extra $3,000 in savings which hasn't been targeted for some specific purpose, and are only contemplating a minor renovation, you're all set. But if you don't have the extra money, and aren't expecting a surprise cash gift of $3,000, you must come up with a way to save it.

Whatever the size of your renovation, start your affordability analysis by compiling a list of where your money goes each month. Take out your checkbook, as many credit card bills as you can find, and your most recent bank statements. Go through them line by line and place each expense into a very specific category. Some will be obvious. How much are your monthly mortgage and property tax payments? How much do you pay for water, gas, and electric, or for home heating oil? If you're not on a balanced billing program, average your past year's utility bills. If you can't find them or your old canceled checks, call the utility or fuel company. They'll be able to calculate the number for you. While you're on the telephone with them, do yourself a favor and sign up for balanced billing. Come up with the same kind of monthly average for your telephone bill as well.

Include any portion of your income that goes to pension funds that you can choose to opt out of. Are you making regular investments or deposits in savings or insurance plans? If so, add the monthly deduction, investment, or deposit to your list as an expense. I'm not saying you should raid these monies. I simply think at this point it's important for you to understand how much is going where.

Next, turn to your insurance premiums. How much do you spend each month on life, auto, health, disability, and homeowners insurance? While you're investigating these areas, tabulate how much of your money each month goes to nonreimbursable medical expenses, auto repairs and fuel, and home maintenance and repair.

Calculate your loan payments. How much is your car loan, or your monthly lease charge? If you or your spouse have any outstanding student loans, write down the amount of the monthly payment. Have you been carrying credit card balances? If so, figure out the amount you spend each month on servicing these debts and how much longer they last.

While you have your credit card statements out, go through them and try to categorize your expenses. Once again, be very specific. How much do you spend on clothing, on restaurants, on gifts, on nonreimbursable travel and entertainment, and on your hobbies each month? Go through your checkbook looking for similar expenses. In addition, look for charitable donations made throughout the year, payments for magazine and newspaper subscriptions, membership dues, fees for professional services, and banking charges, and come up with a monthly average for each.

The numbers you're coming up with may be frightening, but the worst is yet to come. After finishing with your checkbook and credit card statements, take a close look at your bank statements. Figure out how much of your monthly pay you don't deposit, and add to it all the withdrawals you make monthly. Let's call the resulting number "cash expenditures." Obviously, a portion of it goes to food, the one major category we haven't yet calculated. Figure out how much on average you spend on each trip to the supermarket, and multiply that by the number of times you shop for food each month. Add in the incidental trips to the store for milk or bread or coffee.

I'll bet there's still a sizable amount of cash expenditures you can't account for. Where does all the money go? Don't be ashamed if you don't have a ready answer. Most Americans have no idea where about 25 percent of their money goes. They keep a constant one hundred dollars in cash on hand, let's say, and continually replenish it through the month by making frequent withdrawals from automated teller machines. For the moment, put your embarrassment aside and try to determine where the money is actually going. How much do you spend on dry cleaning and trips to the laundromat? How much do you give your children in allowances? How often do you buy stamps? Are you taking taxis and eating lunch out? How often do you go to the movies or rent videos?

Unless the wad in your pocket just keeps getting bigger, or you redeposit it in the bank, all that cash is going somewhere. Wrack your brains to come up with where. Don't take the easy way out and put it all in a miscellaneous category. The more specific you can be about where your money is going, the easier it will be to figure out how much you can spend on this renovation project. That's because we're going to go back through the list and see where you can cut back. The source of your monthly home renovation project will be money you've diverted from other uses (including periodic savings) to put toward a home renovation.

Don't get worried. I know you probably feel like you've

been living from paycheck to paycheck, and there's no room to cut back. But go through those itemized categories and see what you come up with. When you first bought your home you probably were living from hand to mouth, struggling just to pay the bills. But your income has increased since then, and you've already bought most of the furniture and appliances you need. For the past few years you've probably been spending as much on your wants as on your needs. And if you truly want to renovate your home—if it's really important to you—you'll figure out ways of cutting back.

STEP #2: DOWNSIZE YOUR LIFESTYLE AND TRIM EXPENDITURES

That's the next part of the process. Starting at the top of your list and working down, we're going to see how much money we can save by trimming each line. This may seem to be penny-pinching, but it's actually a very important change in attitude. The idea is to reduce your expenditures, and in the process, turn those savings into a home renovation project. You're not so much pinching pennies as you are shifting from a self-centered to a home-centered lifestyle.

There's nothing you can really do about your mortgage payment and property taxes, but how about conserving energy to save on your utility bills. Do you leave lights burning? How high do you set your thermostat? Do you take baths instead of showers? Consider your telephone use. When do you make your long distance calls? Are there any cheaper long distance services available? I realize you're not going to come up with a sizable savings from cutting back on utility and telephone bills. But any cuts you can make in these areas, no matter how minor, will be cuts you don't need to make in other areas. I consider these savings as compensation for the other cuts you'll soon be making. It may only translate into enough money to pay for one dinner out every other month, or an extra present for your child in December, but that's much better than pouring it down the drain.

Turn next to your insurance bills. You'd be surprised at the differences between the premiums charged by various insurers for substantially the same coverage. Contact your broker or agent and ask them to get new bids from solid carriers for all your insurance policies. Stress you're looking for cheaper premiums for the same coverage. Reconsider your deductibles.

I don't recommend switching doctors or going to HMOs to save on nonreimbursable medical bills, or scrimping on auto repairs, but you could start pumping your own gas, or using lower octane fuel. Better yet, you could use your car less often. And while you certainly shouldn't cut back on home repair and maintenance—the whole point of this is to come up with money for your home—you may be able to save some money. Are you paying someone to mow your lawn? Maybe you could find a cheaper gardener, or start doing it yourself. (Yes, cutting the lawn is one thing I think you can do yourself.) Similarly, if you're using a house cleaning service perhaps you can find a cheaper one, or eliminate it entirely.

There's nothing you can do about your student loans, or your existing auto loan payments, but you can resolve not to buy a new car for the next few years, or to select one based on its economy and utility, not its top speed or sexy lines. As for debt service on credit cards—eliminate it. Pay off your outstanding balances as soon as possible, and resolve to stay away from credit cards. The interest charges on credit cards are almost usurious, and since they're not tax-deductible, incurring them is doubly foolish. Keep a single charge card handy for emergencies, but take all the rest of the credit cards out of your wallet and put them in your safe-deposit box. From now on pay cash or write a check for every thing you buy, other than needed big-ticket purchases. You'll be amazed at how much the pain involved in actually laying out cash, or the time it takes to retotal your checking account balance, cuts down on your impulse spending.

The secret is to eliminate all unnecessary spending. Do you really need a new wardrobe every season? Can't you cut down the number of times you go out to dinner? There's no reason you need to buy every newly released compact disk, is there? Instead of flying to Barbados for a week during the winter, why not drive to a national park? And rather than renting a house on the beach during the summer, how about visiting area museums? These lifestyle adjustments will actually be less of a sacrifice than you think. Remember that in exchange for them you'll have a newly renovated home. Time spent at home will be more enjoyable, more comfortable, and more rewarding. You'll be less likely to want to eat out, or escape, if you've an expanded kitchen to cook in and a new family room to relax in.

Be especially ruthless when you're looking to trim cash expenditures. Can you wash and iron your own shirts? How about taking the bus instead of a taxi—or better yet, walking? Rent videos rather than go to the movies—the popcorn is better at home anyway. Buy generic paper products at the supermarket, and become a coupon clipper. Read and compare the unit pricing labels (government mandated stickers which explain how much individual items cost per ounce or per pound) on supermarket shelves and buy the most economical brands. Do everything you can think of to trim your monthly expenses.

For inspiration think back to the stories your parents and grandparents told about scrimping and saving during the Depression. And be grateful that your sacrificing will be rewarded with more than just survival: You'll end up with a more enjoyable and valuable home.

Once you've gone through every expense on your list, go back and start again. Ask yourself one question: what are you willing to give up, to do without, in order to renovate your home. Bear in mind every dollar you save is directly transferable to your home renovation project. After going through the list twice, total your give-ups.

Step #3: To Renovate or To Invest?

Next, take a look at those savings and investment plans you've set up. If your oldest child is ten or younger, I'd give serious thought to converting your monthly tuition savings into a home renovation payment. Similarly, if you've been stashing money away for retirement, and you're less than fifty, consider shifting those monies to the project. In the final analysis, your home is the single best investment you have. It's the only one you have complete control over. And by renovating you may be increasing its value. When the time comes to pay for your child's education, or to retire, you can always come back to the home for financing. By then you'll have paid off whatever type of loan you took out for the renovation, or you'll have built up additional equity allowing you to once again refinance. Meanwhile, you'll have made your life and the lives of your family more comfortable, enjoyable, and pleasurable.

Besides, you can assume your income will continue to

increase, so eventually, you'll be able once again to start setting money aside. Even though there may be periods in your life in which your income stagnates or perhaps even decreases due to external economic conditions, over the long term I firmly believe most people's income will increase. That's because the more experienced you are the better your work performance will be, and the better your performance the more you'll earn. Of course this assumes you won't allow yourself to be derailed by foolish employers, short-sighted job interviewers, or your own complacency. However, if you feel in immediate peril on the job, it's not the time to be spending money on a home renovation. Still, it makes sense to go through the same cost-cutting exercises. Any savings you can make in your monthly spending will strengthen your safety net and give you more time to look for another job if need be.

Add any available monthly investment or deposit figures to your total of give-ups. The resulting sum is how much you can afford to spend each month, on top of your current mortgage payment, for a home renovation.

That doesn't mean you can't stretch further still if need be. You can also use past savings you've accumulated as a one-time cash payment. Consider it the equivalent of a down payment on a home. If you've some money sitting in the bank, earning interest at a rate slightly above the rate of inflation, it may make sense to use it for a renovation.

Despite the recent recession, well-situated and cared for homes have over the long term increased in value at a rate of one to two percentage points ahead of inflation. If the annual inflation rate is 4 percent your home will increase in value 6 percent each year. Assuming you renovate intelligently, with an eye toward simultaneously increasing your pleasure and the value of the home, a renovation investment may make more sense than a nonequity mutual fund.

If, for example, you have $10,000 earning 6 percent interest in a certificate of deposit, you can theoretically "earn" the same interest by investing it in your home. And you'll also be able to enjoy the fruits of that $10,000 investment—your newly renovated home. Granted, your investment isn't as liquid, but I think that's outweighed by the lifestyle enhancement. Only you can decide how much that enhancement is worth. Is it worth giving up 1 percent interest a year? I think so. How about 2 percent? Maybe. What if the difference is 3 percent? Now I'm starting to have qualms. If you've $10,000 in the bank earning 9 percent interest I might, I repeat might, advise you to keep it there. But the decision is yours alone. Only you know how much a renovated home will mean to you and your family.

A chart on page 76 illustrates this concept graphically. The bottom arrow is the inflation rate. The arrow directly above it represents the increase in value of your home. As you can see it is fixed at around two points higher than inflation. The uppermost arrow represents interest earned on investments. Unlike an investment in your own home, it varies relative to inflation. The gap between the middle arrow (investment in your home) and the top arrow (interest rates) is the gray area in your calculations. Is the size of this gap made up for by the added lifestyle benefits a home renovation will bring to your family? Or is it too high a price to pay for a little bit of luxury or some additional living space? Only you can make that decision.

In order to translate your monthly numbers into a renovation budget, you need to figure out how you'll be financing your projects. The decision generally depends on how much equity you have in your home, and how expensive your project turns out to be.

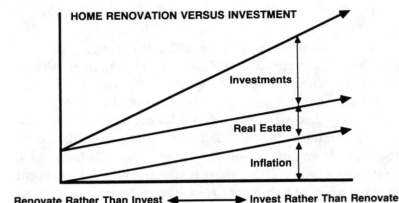

FINANCING OPTION #1: INSTALLMENT LOANS

Projects costing between $3,000 and $10,000 are best financed with installment loans. If the loan is specifically intended for the renovation of a home, and is secured by the home itself, it's called a home improvement loan. If the loan in unsecured, and relies solely on your income and credit history, the bank will call it a personal loan and won't stipulate what it's to be used for. Of course, the interest charges on unsecured personal loans are substantially higher than on secured home improvement loans. The interest charges on installment loans secured by your home are tax-deductible. The payments for secured installment loans may be spread out over five to seven years. The payments for unsecured loans last from one to three years. Installment loans are fairly easy to obtain. Banks are aggressive in their issuing of them, since the short terms and high interest rates make them very profitable.

But the very things that make them advantageous to banks make them painful to consumers. Short terms plus hefty interest equals sizable monthly payments. If you find the payments exceed your monthly affordability, investigate the Department of Housing and Urban Development's Title I program. This federally sponsored program enables some banks to offer fifteen-year home improvement loans. The extended term reduces the monthly payments dramatically. Your income must fall within certain parameters, however, and your renovation must meet federal guidelines for being a nonluxury project.

Financing Option #2: Borrowing on Equity

If your renovation work will cost more than $10,000 the best thing to do will be to borrow against the equity you have in your home. Your equity is equal to the difference between your home's current market value and the balance of your mortgage. If your home is today worth $200,000, and you have a balance of $150,000 left to pay off, you have $50,000 worth of equity. If you've no equity in your home you'll be forced to rely on an expensive, and nondeductible, personal loan.

I'll use Michael and Barbara Newparent again to help explain how equity lending works. They bought their home around ten years ago for $100,000. At that time, they put down $20,000 cash, and a bank put up the other $80,000. While they took possession of the home, they were actually only 20 percent owners. In the past ten years, however, they've been paying the bank off each month. For the first five years, those payments didn't make much of a dent in the actual $80,000, since they were mostly interest, but since then they've been cutting into the principal. At the same time, the value of their home has been increasing. Rather than being worth $100,000, thanks to inflation it's worth $130,000 today. Their paying down the mortgage loan and the increase in their home's value offer opportunities to borrow more money to pay for a renovation project.

Since the Newparents' home is worth $130,000 today, and they have $70,000 of their mortgage left to pay off, they have $60,000 worth of equity. For the same reasons a bank thinks it's wise to leverage the initial 80 percent of the value of a home, it considers it prudent to allow a homeowner to bring their leverage back up to 80 percent. Banks will look at the new loan and the original mortgage as a package. For example: Since the Newparents' home is now worth $130,000, banks will let them carry up to 80 percent of that, or $104,000, in debt. Since they still owe $70,000 on their first mortgage, banks will let them borrow up to $34,000 ($104,000 minus $70,000) in a home-equity loan. The actual amount would be less, since application, financing, and processing charges would be tacked on. The home-equity lender need not be the same bank that lent the first $80,000, and the exact amount they'll lend will also depend on the borrower's ability to meet the monthly payments and the bank's policies. Many, for instance, will only allow a homeowner to leverage 75 percent of their home's value through a second mortgage. In addition, keep in mind the Internal Revenue Service will only allow you to deduct the interest on up to $100,000 of home-equity debt (a second mortgage).

Some more aggressive banks have a variation on this loan that takes into account that the renovation itself may increase the value of a home. The banks will study the renovation plans and base their appraisal of a home's current value on what it will be worth after the renovation is finished. Let's go back to the house the Newparents bought ten years ago for $100,000. It may be worth $130,000 today, but after the renovation it will be worth $150,000.

That means they would have $80,000, not $60,000, worth of equity. These aggressive banks will loan them up to $50,000 (80 percent of $150,000, minus the $70,000 remaining on their first mortgage), not just $34,000 (80 percent of $130,000, minus $70,000). There are a couple of hitches, however. First, the banks won't actually give the Newparents the money until after the renovation has been completed. That means they'll need to make some other short-term financing arrangements using the bank's commitment as collateral in order to pay the bills. And second, the bank will only do this if the Newparents are "valued customers." That's usually a euphemism for big or long-term depositors. So unless you've a great deal of money or experience in a particular bank, don't expect this type of service.

These loans are called different things depending on how the money will be paid out and how interest will be charged. If you opt simply to receive a check for the amount, interest will accrue on the entire sum immediately and it will be called a home-equity loan. You will receive monthly payment stubs just like for any other timed loan. If you decide you'd rather draw the money as you need it, interest will accrue only on what you draw out, and it will be called a home-equity line of credit. Banks offer two different ways for you to gain access to home-equity lines of credit: either through a special checkbook or with a special credit card. The straight-loan form is better if you want a set monthly payment and if your project is scheduled to last only a short period of time. If you'll be involved in a long project stretching out months rather than weeks, or if you intend to renovate your home through a series of separate smaller projects over an extended period of time, a home-equity line of credit may be more convenient and end up costing less in interest.

FINANCING OPTION #3: REFINANCING YOUR MORTGAGE

Another option would be to refinance your first mortgage. Most people think of mortgage refinancing as a way to decrease monthly payments, but it can also be used to pull your equity money back out of the house. The concept is called "cashing out." Let's go back to the Newparents. Ten years ago they bought their home for $100,000. They put $20,000 down and took out a thirty-year, $80,000 mortgage. Today their home is worth $130,000 and they've paid their mortgage down to $70,000. If they turned to a bank and asked to refinance their mortgage, it would offer to loan them up to 75 percent of its value in a refinanced mortgage. (Some will only go up to 65 percent.) That means it will let them borrow up to $97,500, depending on their meeting the bank's other qualifications. After paying off the remaining $70,000 on their previous mortgage they'd be left with $27,500 (less any application, processing, and financing charges) that could be used to finance a home renovation. The tax ramifications of mortgage refinancing vary depending on the exact numbers and use of funds. Check with your tax advisor for information on how it would affect your tax bill.

Deciding which financing method to choose isn't just a matter of calculating which will provide the most funds. Your first concern is monthly affordability. Home-equity loans and home-equity lines of credit generally have shorter terms (generally from ten to twenty years) and higher interest rates than first mortgages. By refinancing you're actually obtaining another first mortgage. If you refinance your interest will be lower and you'll have up to thirty more years to pay it off. In order to compare monthly charges, add your current mortgage payment to the potential home-equity loan payment, and match it with the proposed payment of a refinanced mortgage. Next, consider the duration of the loans. Refinancing is a long-term obligation—even longer than your original mortgage. Home-equity borrowing, on the other hand, is shorter term—the debt may be paid off in ten years. Depending on your stage in life, and what other obligations may be on the horizon (college tuition?, elder care?), you may not want to commit yourself to a thirty-year debt. Examine which method will yield the most funds. If you're stretching to pay for the renovation of your dreams, you may need to bite the bullet in order to get the most money possible. Finally, look at the costs involved in the actual borrowing. The up-front costs involved in refinancing are higher than in borrowing against your equity.

WEIGHING THE OPTIONS

Let's see how the Newparents weighed their choices and came up with a budget. Since they have some equity in their home, the Newparents know they won't need to take out a personal loan. After going through their expenses they know they can afford to spend $250 a month, on top of their current $825 a month mortgage payment. And if needed they're willing to use their savings of $5,000. Because they have no firm idea of what their dream project will cost, they decide to figure out what they could afford to borrow with a home improvement loan, a home-equity loan, and through refinancing their mortgage. Barbara calls a nearby savings bank to find out the current rates on all three loans. She learns the bank is now charging 9.5 percent on thirty-year first mortgages, 11 percent on twenty-year home-equity loans, and 14 percent on five-year home improvement loans.

Michael finds the page with the chart for 14 percent

loans in a book of mortgage charts he purchased at the neighborhood book store. (These books are readily available and are commonly called "mortgage books.") He runs down the five-year-term column until he finds the payment closest to $250. He sees that a monthly payment of $232.68 will enable them to borrow $10,000. If they add in their $5,000 worth of savings that means they can afford a $15,000 renovation if they choose a home improvement loan. Next, he finds the page for 11 percent loans. Running down the twenty-year-term column he finds a monthly payment of $251.81, which translates into a home-equity loan of $25,000. He adds their $5,000 savings to that to come up with a potential budget of $30,000 if they take out a home-equity loan. Finally he turns to the page of 9.5 percent loans. Since they're already paying $825 per month, and can afford another $250 per month, he looks down the thirty-year-term column for the payment closest to $1,075. He finds that with a monthly payment of $1093.11 they could afford to refinance their home with another $130,000 mortgage. But since a bank would only let them borrow $97,500, and they would need to pay off the remaining $70,000 on their previous mortgage, a refinancing would yield $27,500. Adding in their $5,000 savings would bring that up to $32,500. Even though a mortgage refinancing would yield more money, the Newparents decide the difference isn't enough to justify the added up-front costs and the additional ten-year obligation. They decide to budget their job at $25,000, and hold the additional $5,000 in savings aside in case more is needed.

Of course, the Newparents' situation is a hypothetical case. Your situation may justify refinancing your mortgage, or simply taking out a home improvement loan. Just as I don't recommend you serve as your own general contractor, I don't believe you should make such an important decision on your own. Speak with your financial advisor. Tell her your thoughts and fears, and get her input and advice. If necessary, have her work out the numbers for you. But remember, in the end, the decision will be yours.

WORKSHEET FOR HOME RENOVATION AFFORDABILITY

This is a worksheet to help you make all the affordability calculations I discussed in this chapter. In the first column you'll find a list of all the areas in which you are spending money each month. After calculating how much you spend in each category, write that number in the second column. Then, figure out how much you can save and write that number in the third column. Subtract the savings in column three from the current spending in column two and write the result, your new monthly spending figure, in the fourth column. Then total up all the columns. Next, subtract the total of your new monthly expenses from your monthly take-home pay. The difference is how much you can afford to spend each month on a home renovation.

Category	Monthly Expenses		Savings		New Monthly Expenses
Mortgage	_____	–	_____	=	_____
Property taxes	_____	–	_____	=	_____
Utilities	_____	–	_____	=	_____
Telephone	_____	–	_____	=	_____
Pension plan	_____	–	_____	=	_____
Savings plan	_____	–	_____	=	_____
Investment plan	_____	–	_____	=	_____

Life insurance	_____	–	_____	=	_____
Auto insurance	_____	–	_____	=	_____
Health insurance	_____	–	_____	=	_____
Home insurance	_____	–	_____	=	_____
Disability insurance	_____	–	_____	=	_____
Nonreimbursable medical	_____	–	_____	=	_____
Auto repairs	_____	–	_____	=	_____
Auto fuel	_____	–	_____	=	_____
Home repair	_____	–	_____	=	_____
Car payment	_____	–	_____	=	_____
Student loan(s)	_____	–	_____	=	_____
Debt service	_____	–	_____	=	_____
Clothing	_____	–	_____	=	_____
Restaurants	_____	–	_____	=	_____
Gifts	_____	–	_____	=	_____
Nonreimbursable travel and entertainment	_____	–	_____	=	_____
Hobbies	_____	–	_____	=	_____
Charitable donations	_____	–	_____	=	_____
Subscriptions	_____	–	_____	=	_____
Membership dues	_____	–	_____	=	_____

Professional services	_____	–	_____	=	_____
Banking charges	_____	–	_____	=	_____
Food	_____	–	_____	=	_____
Dry cleaning/ laundry	_____	–	_____	=	_____
Allowances	_____	–	_____	=	_____
Postage	_____	–	_____	=	_____
Taxis	_____	–	_____	=	_____
Lunches out	_____	–	_____	=	_____
Movies and videos	_____	–	_____	=	_____
Total	_____	–	_____	=	_____
Total monthly income					_____
Total new monthly expenses			–		_____
Monthly renovation affordability				=	_____

Equity/Refinancing Assessment

The following worksheet will help you determine whether you should take out a home-equity loan or refinance your mortgage in order to finance a home renovation. By following this equation you'll be able to see which method will yield the most funds. However, as I mentioned in the text, that is only one variable. After the numerical calculations I have again listed the other variables to consider when choosing between home-equity loans and mortgage refinancing.

1. Home's current market value   _____
2. Balance of mortgage   _____
3. Your equity (line 1 minus line 2)   _____
4. Line 1 × 80%   _____
5. Maximum home-equity loan (line 4 minus line 2)   _____
6. Line 1 × 75%   _____
7. Maximum refinancing yield (line 6 minus line 2)   _____
8. Available cash   _____
9. Maximum equity loan budget (line 5 plus line 8)   _____
10. Maximum refinanced budget (line 7 plus line 8)   _____

Other Variables	Home-Equity Loan	Mortgage Refinancing
Length of term	10–20 years	20–30 years
Interest	Higher	Lower
Up-front costs	Lower	Higher

CHAPTER 4

Stretching Through Savvy Scheduling

—

Remember that time is money.
—BENJAMIN FRANKLIN

With a clear idea of what you want done, and how much you can afford to spend, you have all you need to start committing your renovation project to paper. But that doesn't mean you should do so right away. Before you move from your own head out into the world to get the renovation process started, you should give some thought to the timing of your project.

The home renovation industry, like most others, is seasonal. From April to September general contractors and subcontractors are very busy. The warmer weather makes for better outdoor working conditions, and leads homeowners to give more thought to renovation projects. According to U.S. Department of Commerce studies, illustrated graphically below, contractors do 58 percent of their yearly business from April through September. The slowest months are January, February, and March, when contractors do only 18 percent of their annual business. During these slow periods, prices should drop, since contractors are anxious for any business. That means you'll save money by making sure your project is scheduled for this slow period. You'll also have the best chance of having the general contractor give your job her undivided, or nearly undivided, attention.

Of course, if you live in the northern third of the country and your project is external in nature, a general contractor may discourage you from scheduling it in the winter months. Try your best, however, to insist on a winter schedule. Unless the ground is frozen and your job requires excavation, any project, interior or exterior, can be

MONTHLY TRENDS IN THE RENOVATION INDUSTRY

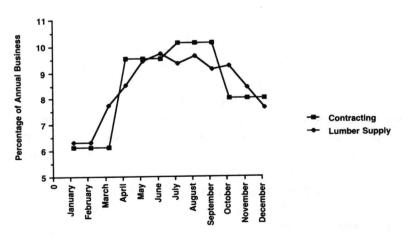

Source: U.S. Department of Commerce

done during January, February, and March. You may even be able to have the excavation work done in advance, perhaps in mid-December. It may not be as convenient for the general contractor and her crew—they may need to wear down vests and flannel shirts rather than just T-shirts—but it will be more economical for you.

In order to take advantage of the lull in the industry you need to establish and stick to a fairly rigid schedule from day one. Generally speaking, it means you must begin the process anywhere from eight to twelve months in advance. The exact length of time depends on the type of project. The more complex a job is, the longer the lead time. That's because you'll need more time to hammer out the details of your plans and specifications.

I'll discuss the specifics of selecting a planning professional in the next chapter. For now, suffice it to say that if you're planning an extensive renovation you'll be working with an architect or designer; if your job consists solely of the cosmetic face-lift of a kitchen or bathroom you'll need a designer or space planner; and if your project is simply a system upgrade you'll be hiring a home inspector.

Plan on taking at least one month to find, interview, and select the planner who's right for you, regardless of which professional you use. If you're using an architect or designer, you'll need to set aside at least six months to work with them on the plans. You'll need about four months to work with a space planner on the design for a single room. On the other hand, it will take two months, at most, to make sure the specifications drawn up by a home inspector are complete.

It will then take two months to find, interview, investigate, solicit and analyze bids, and select a general contractor. Then you'll need another month to iron out the details of your contract with her and arrange financing for the project. Assume the general contractor won't actually be able to start work for one to two months after signing the contract.

Let's go back to our hypothetical couples and see what their schedules should be. Michael and Barbara Newparent, the young couple who need to expand their small house, will be working with an architect. So will Bob and Fran Emptynester, who are transforming their characterless colonial into a Georgian with a master bedroom suite and home office. John and Beth Greyhare, who are modernizing their kitchen first, will be using a space planner. And Dave Handeman and Tom Oldehouse, whose home requires some repair and system upgrading, need to hire an inspector. Assume they all have a target starting date of February 1. That means the Newparents and Emptynesters need to begin the process exactly one year ahead of time—February. The Greyhares, who must set aside ten months, should start looking for a space planner in April. Handeman and Oldehouse, on the other hand, can wait until June to find an inspector.

Obviously, renovation schedules aren't like space shuttle missions—there's room for some error. It may only take you five weeks to find an architect, but eight months to hammer out the plans. Your search for a general contractor could take three rather than two months, and she might not be able to start for another three months. Or conversely, you could line up an inspector and finish the specifications in less than a month, and select a general contractor who can start right away. You may want to adjust your schedule to take into account an expected salary bonus or other financial windfall. Perhaps you'll need to work around an important pending social event—like a wedding—or another major expense, such as a previously arranged vacation. Don't worry. If a job starts in January or March, or

December or April, rather than in February, its cost won't suddenly jump 15 or 25 percent. The idea is simply to do everything humanly possible to fit your project into the contractors' slow period, and therefore maximize your chances of getting the best price.

If for some reason you can't spend the necessary time on a project you have two choices: either cut corners to get it in under deadline, or postpone it until you have the time. I'd advise the latter course. Rushing a renovation is a recipe for disaster. Even if it means selling your home without repairing the roof, and getting a lower price because of it, you're better off letting the new owners deal with it themselves than rushing and spending money on a poor job.

SAMPLE SCHEDULES

The following are three sample schedules detailing exactly how far in advance of actually having the work done in February (general contractors' slowest month) you should begin the renovation process, and what you should be doing each month. The first schedule assumes an extensive project such as a space addition or a remodeling, based on plans and specifications drawn up by an architect or interior designer. The second schedule is based on a project that is primarily a cosmetic face-lift (redoing a bathroom or kitchen for example) and uses the services of an interior designer or space planner. The third schedule is for a relatively less complex project such as a system upgrade or the addition of a single amenity, using a home inspector to draft job specifications. If several system upgrades are taking place simultaneously, or if the amenities are part of a larger project, refer to either of the other two schedules.

SPACE ADDITIONS AND REMODELING PROJECTS
(using an architect or designer)

February:
• solicit names of architects or designers
• interview candidates
• select one
• work out contract

March through August:
• work with architect or designer in developing comprehensive set of plans and specifications
• study the model or the sketches
• do preliminary research on financing options

September and October:
• select financing option
• solicit names of general contractors
• investigate them and their subcontractors
• obtain bids from three candidates
• analyze bids
• select one

November:
• work out details of contract with general contractor
• obtain financing for project

December and January:
• general contractor finishes other projects, freeing up schedule

February:
• work begins

COSMETIC FACE-LIFT PROJECTS
(using a space planner or designer)

April:
- find and interview space planners or designers
- select one
- work out arrangement with them and/or showroom

May through August:
- work with space planner or designer in developing comprehensive set of plans and specifications

September and October:
- solicit names of general contractors
- investigate them and their subcontractors
- obtain bids from three candidates
- analyze bids
- select one

November:
- work out details of contract with general contractor
- obtain financing for project

December and January:
- general contractor finishes other projects, freeing up schedule

February:
- work begins

SYSTEM UPGRADE OR INDIVIDUAL LUXURY ADDITION
(using a home inspector)

June:
- solicit names of home inspectors

- interview candidates
- select one
- work out contract

July and August:
- work with home inspector in developing comprehensive set of specifications

September and October:
- solicit names of general contractors
- investigate them and their subcontractors
- obtain bids from three candidates
- analyze bids
- select one

November:
- work out details of contract with general contractor
- obtain financing for project

December and January:
- general contractor finishes other projects, freeing up schedule

February:
- work begins

CHAPTER 5

Designs, Plans, and Specifications

———

A danger foreseen is half avoided.
—THOMAS FULLER

I firmly believe that in order for a home renovation to work smoothly you'll need to have in your hands, as early as possible, a comprehensive description of the renovation project—a blueprint for the job. While the form and author of this blueprint will vary depending on the type and size of the project, it's a requirement for every job from the smallest repair to the most grand remodeling. Having a comprehensive set of plans and specifications accomplishes four things: it insures your wants and needs—not those of the general contractor—are expressed in the design; it reasonably insures bids won't be out of line with your budget; it allows competitive bids to be compared, analyzed, and validated; and it guarantees attention will be paid to the aesthetic sense of the structure.

The single biggest mistake made in home renovation is having the same person plan and execute the work. Unfortunately, it's also the most common mistake. Let's go back to Fran and Bob Emptynester, the couple who want to remodel their characterless colonial. They've decided they want to gut the second floor, taking the current three bedroom/one bathroom layout and converting it into a master bedroom/master bathroom and guest room/guest bathroom plan. They call in three general contractors—two recommended by neighbors and one whose name Bob got from the Yellow Pages—explain what they want, and ask for bids. The three general contractors listen to the Emptynesters' sketchy notions of how they envision the completed second floor, and try to translate these dreams into wood and Sheetrock and dollars and cents.

But that's not what a general contractor is trained to do. That's the role of a design or planning professional. Since they're not schooled in design, general contractors reach back into their past for a similar job, and simply replicate it. Or worse yet, they wing it. Even though they too would end up being better off, none of the three general contractors will turn to the Emptynesters and say, "You should hire an architect to draw up plans." That's because the general contractors don't want to have someone looking over their shoulder, dictating what they should and shouldn't be doing, and standing between them and the Emptynesters.

The end result is that the general contractors prepare bids that aren't comparable. All three have reached different solutions for how to redivide the second floor space. Only one has been careful to consider the outside appearance of the house. Another general contractor specified very expensive granite in the bathrooms—Fran mentioned she liked granite—and included the cost of new light fixtures. The third simply went back and calculated how much it cost him per square foot to build a dormer last month, multiplied that figure by the square footage of the Emptynesters' job, and finagled the bid to back into his number.

Even though it's like comparing apples to oranges, the Emptynesters match the bids up against each other. The bidding sheets are like gibberish to them, so all they really get from the paperwork is the bottom line—the estimated cost. The Emptynesters consider how they feel about the three contractors: who do they like best?; who seems the most experienced?; who do they have the most confidence in?; and whose ideas are the most interesting? In other words, they're letting themselves be sold, rather than proactively buying; they're selecting the best salesman rather than the best general contractor from among the three general contractors.

Rather than choosing the person best suited to take *their* vision of what they want done to their home and give it form, the Emptynesters are handing complete control over the job to the individual whose personality they like best. And in the process, assuming that because they like this general contractor best, he or she will have taste like their own. It would be laughable if it weren't so common. The Emptynesters should have commissioned an architect or designer to draft a detailed set of plans for the remodeling project, which included specific information on both the floor plan and the materials to be used, and then had the general contractors bid on it.

The need for a comprehensive set of plans and specifications extends beyond remodeling jobs to other types of projects as well. The same would hold true for Michael and Barbara Newparent, our hypothetical couple who want an addition to their two-bedroom home. Or for John and Beth Greyhare, who are adding a deck as the first step in transforming their family homestead into a retirement home. Even homeowners who are upgrading a home system would be foolish to begin the project without a comprehensive written description of the work to be done. Let's go back to Dave Handeman and Tom Oldehouse who own the home needing some systems work.

They decide they're going to work on the exterior of their home first; they'll invest in a new roof, vinyl siding, and new gutters and downspouts. Dave asks his friends at work for the names of general contractors and gets two names, and Tom sees a contractor at work on a home a few blocks away and takes down the telephone number. The three general contractors stop over at the house, look around, climb up on the roof, bang on the clapboards a few times, and leave to compile their bids. Two days later, the bids are dropped off at the house. Dave and Tom look them over. One bid is dramatically lower than the others. It happens to be from the contractor currently working in the area. Tom walks over to the other job, looks around, bangs on the siding, finds it tight, and leaves satisfied. The next day Dave calls and schedules the project.

Dave and Tom don't realize the reasons why this bid was much lower than the others. The low-priced general contractor has based his estimates on using lesser quality materials than the other two general contractors. He'll be installing lightweight asphalt shingles, which aren't as durable or fire resistant as those the other general contractors were going to use. The gutters and downspouts will be of a thinner aluminum, and he won't be changing the configuration of gutters and downspouts to eliminate the current drainage problems. Finally, Tom's finding that the vinyl siding on the previous job was tight indicates shoddy, not quality workmanship—it should actually hang loose so it can expand and contract. While the project may end up being an improvement over what they now have, Dave and Tom are getting a roof, gutters, and siding that won't last as long as they should. But because they know nothing about quality materials or workmanship all they have to go by is price.

That's because the bids obtained weren't comparable since there were no specifications for the job. The general contractors made their own estimates of what was required, and bid on them. Instead, Dave and Tom should have had a simple list of specifications prepared that stated the type and quality of materials to be used in the project, and what modifications should be made, and then lined up someone knowledgeable to make sure the work was done correctly.

Having a set of comprehensive plans and specifications is actually as important to the general contractor as it is to the homeowner. When it comes time to solicit bids you'll be insisting the general contractors come in with a fixed, or binding, price—known in the industry as a budget price. That way you'll know exactly what the final bill will be. That means the general contractors will need to be very sure of the size and scope of the job. They'll need to be able to make accurate projections of how much time, labor, and material will be required. And then they'll need to factor in their overhead, profit, and a comfortable cushion to compensate for potential problems. Without a full set of plans, no general contractor can give you a budget price; therefore, you'll have no idea of what the job will end up costing.

Having a set of plans and specifications eliminates the

surprise element of projects' costs—or at least it should. By beginning with a general budget, and having plans and specifications drawn up based on that budget, you maximize your chances to have the project actually come in close to the price level you initially project. A seasoned professional should be able to provide plans and specifications that will come within 15 percent of your budget. And if your budget is extremely tight, you can always consider telling them a little white lie, and saying your budget is 15 percent less than it actually is.

I'm using the phrase "plans and specifications" to refer to a wide range of forms. In its broadest sense it refers to a package of documents prepared by an architect, including what are individually known as plans, specifications, elevations, sections, and detailings. Plans are an overhead look at the floor plan of each level of the home. Specifications are a list of characteristics and features, which may include the types, weights, colors, and sizes of materials or fixtures. Elevations are ground-level views of the front, rear, and both sides of the structure. Sections are cross sectional views of the home, seen as though the house was sliced down a particular line. Detailings are sketches of particular, usually complex, ornamental or structural parts of the project—a special cornice molding for example. (Three-dimensional models and perspective drawings aren't included in a set of plans—they cost extra.)

Depending on the size and complexity of the project in question the plans and specifications package may include all or even just one of the above elements. The Emptynesters' remodeling project, and the Newparents' addition will both probably require a full set of documents. The Greyhares' deck, however, may only require a single overhead plan, one elevation, and a specifications list. For Dave Handeman and Tom Oldehouse's exterior upgrading project all that would be required is a specifications list.

One element that should be included in every plans and specifications package is job supervision. Simply having a comprehensive plan is useless, unless you know that the general contractor is actually doing what the plan requires. In most cases, the best person to insure that the plan is being followed to the letter is the person who drew up the plan in the first place. Dave Handeman and Tom Oldehouse may develop a long list of specifications for the type of shingles they want used on their roof and the type of siding they want installed on their outside walls, but neither of them have the knowledge or skill to determine whether or not those specifications are actually being followed by the general contractor. How much supervision is actually necessary, and what that entails, varies with the size and complexity of the job. For smaller and simpler projects it may simply involve a handful of trips to the job site to insure that the proper materials are being used and that the work is proceeding as it should. In large and complex projects there may need to be daily supervision, including keeping tabs on the work of the general contractor and individual subcontractors, as well as deliveries of material and fixtures.

Who you commission to draft these plans and specifications and supervise your project depends on what type of job you're having done. As I mentioned earlier in the book, home renovations generally fall into one of five categories: remodeling, space additions, cosmetic face-lifts, system upgrades, and luxury additions. If you are remodeling or adding space to your home you'll need to hire an architect to prepare your plans and specifications. In most remodeling projects and space additions the architect can also provide job supervision. But in extremely large and complex projects you should bring in a separate supervisory professional called a construction manager. If your project is a cosmetic face-lift, you should hire an interior designer to both draft the plans and supervise the job. And if you are upgrading a home system, or having an amenity added, a home inspector should be commissioned to provide specifications and supervision.

ARCHITECTS

Americans have a host of misconceptions about architects. We think of them as visionaries, walking a fine line between genius and insanity, obsessed with building monumental works, and concerned only with the big picture. In other words, we believe all architects are like Howard Roarke from Ayn Rand's novel *The Fountainhead*.

Not only aren't all architects visionaries, only a select minority work on monumental buildings. Most architects design average size buildings and homes. Some even spend their time designing play structures and garages. We often forget almost every home originated on some architect's drawing board. It's only because certain styles have become ubiquitous that we now associate architects with one of a kind, estatelike homes.

Architects are also, despite common misconceptions, very concerned with details. It was an architect, Mies van der Rohe, who, when talking about inspiration and design, said "God is in the details." A good architect is just as concerned with the size, texture, and colors of the tiles in a bathroom as she is with the facade of a house. They're also very interested in renovation work. While it may not be as rewarding as designing a home from scratch, it can be a challenge to add space to a home without destroying its character, or to add character to a home that lacked it previously. And in addition to the challenge, it pays the bills. There just aren't enough people and businesses commissioning designs of entire homes or buildings to support all the architects in the country.

Architects should be used to plan all remodeling and space addition projects for two reasons. First, in most municipalities, any time you are going to move or add a wall the local building department must be notified. Then, before work can begin a permit must be issued. The signature of an architect on the application for a building permit is often an imprimatur for the local building department. Having architecturally drawn plans will help eliminate any potential bureaucratic hassles. Second, and more important, architects are uniquely qualified to make both structural and aesthetic decisions. Remodeling projects and space additions involve both the structure of your home and its aesthetics. When the Emptynesters remodel the second floor of their home they will be tearing down and rearranging weight-bearing walls, as well as changing the facade. And when the Newparents add on to their small two-bedroom house they will be altering both its structural characteristics and aesthetics. That's why both couples should seek out architects.

The best way to find architects and designers is through personal recommendations. Try to speak with people who are in basically the same socioeconomic group as you are. That should insure the fees and tastes of those who are recommended won't be beyond your ability to pay. Once you have a list of names, run them past your local building department. While they may not offer a direct recommendation, you'll at least be able to get a sense of whether they are known and respected by the building department. You don't want to hire someone who's anathema to the building department no matter how brilliant their plans are. If you live in a condominium or cooperative, you may want to consult with the managing agent, building board, or homeowner's association for the same reason.

Interview each candidate who's still on your list. Architects should be members of the American Institute of Architects (AIA). Don't be surprised or turned off if not all of your candidates are licensed. Many excellent architects aren't licensed, since the licensing examination is very strenuous and all it adds to an architect's arsenal of professional skills is the right to sign and file official plans. These unlicensed architects do everything licensed architects do, but when it comes time to sign and file the plans, they simply turn to a colleague who is licensed—often someone sitting in the next office. If it comes down to a toss-up between a licensed architect and an unlicensed architect, opt for the one with the license, but otherwise, don't give the credential too much weight.

More importantly, ask each candidate what percentage of their practice involves residential work and what percentage of that involves renovations. Find out if the individual you're interviewing will actually be doing the work, or whether it will be done by an associate or staff member. If you are the owner of a condominium or cooperative, ask for information about their insurance coverage, since your building board or managing agent may have minimum requirements. Ask if the architect has experience with your style of home. Double-check that they have experience with the local building department or zoning board. And certainly ask about fees and what services go along with them.

Most architects will charge a fee equal to 15 percent of the total cost of the job. This includes job supervision and a full set of plans and specifications. (A model will generally cost you an additional $250, and three-dimensional drawings will typically cost another $100.) I'm not in favor of paying fees based on the cost of the job itself. After all, does an architect expend less energy and put less effort into designing a $20,000 addition than a $200,000 remodeling job? I hope not. The only difference in the jobs should be the time involved; so why not pay them an hourly fee?

Some architects will agree to an hourly arrangement when pressed. But many architects claim clients, while initially happier with an hourly fee, end up more upset than if they opted for a percentage fee. It seems many homeowners don't believe the architect actually spent as much time on the job as she billed, failing to realize there's cerebration involved in addition to the time spent consulting and then physically drawing the plans. If you can get them to agree to an hourly fee grab it. But don't give up on an otherwise acceptable architect because she won't cave in. The hourly rate for services is generally between $55 to $150 per hour for an experienced architect. However the fee is going to be calculated, insist on a cap that can only be exceeded on your specific approval.

Make sure to explain your budget to each candidate architect, and point out how carefully you've come up with it. There are some architects who hate to be constrained by budgetary limits and will promise only to come within the ballpark. But one of your reasons for obtaining detailed plans and specifications is to help you stick to your budget. If a candidate architect balks at monetary restraints, or is uncomfortable about his or her ability to come within 15 percent of your proposed budget, scratch them off your list.

Primarily you are looking for someone who has experience with jobs similar to yours; who seems professional; who has good references; and with whom you feel a certain rapport. I can't overemphasize the importance of rapport between a homeowner and an architect. Their job is to translate your visions and feelings into a workable set of plans—basically, to give substance to your dreams. He or she can steer you, edit your ideas, and point out possibilities, but they should never force their own vision on you. You want someone who shows respect for your ideas and feelings and takes them into account when drawing up plans.

That's why I discourage my clients from hiring famous architects. If you hire a "name" person be prepared for them to nod knowingly at your ideas, and then submit a design that's their vision, not yours. Well-known architects become well known because they have a certain recognizable style—not because they are wonderful at translating clients' visions into reality. If you hire a well-known architect you'll get their style, not yours.

CONSTRUCTION MANAGERS

While architects traditionally include a charge for job supervision in their fee, they are really not construction experts. They learn nothing about the building process in school, so whatever knowledge they possess on the subject is gathered through experience. Still, their ability to verify that the work is being done according to their plans and specifications, and up to traditional standards, will be sufficient supervision for most projects. But on very large jobs, involving more than $100,000 worth of work, I believe it pays to have a real expert on construction work representing your interests.

Such major renovations require hands-on, day-to-day supervision, since even minor problems and delays can mean thousands of dollars down the drain. Architects have neither the knowledge nor the time to provide such constant supervision. Instead, you'll need to call in a construction manager. These professionals have been very common in commercial construction for years and are just now beginning to enter the top-end residential market.

For a fee of between 3 and 5 percent of the total cost, or for between $75 and $100 per hour, they'll serve as your representative on the site, overseeing and checking up on the general contractor. They'll handle everything from analyzing the bids and negotiating the contract with the general contractor, to making sure the right materials are used and are delivered on time.

The best sources for names of construction managers are your candidate architects. While interviewing them, explain that you're contemplating hiring a construction manager and ask for some recommendations. Interview each suggested construction manager and ask about their relevant experience, fees, and services. When in doubt, opt for the construction manager with the most experience in residential renovation.

If you will be using a construction manager, it makes sense to ask the architect to lower their fee, since they won't be providing job supervision, and charge you solely for their design work.

INTERIOR DESIGNERS

If your project is a cosmetic face-life that doesn't involve either the exterior facade or internal structure of your home you should hire an interior designer to draw up plans and specifications and provide job supervision.

Americans have just as many misconceptions about interior designers as they do about architects. The common image of an interior designer is a somewhat pretentious individual who has exquisite but ornate and expensive taste who helps wealthy people furnish their homes. The problem is, that's a caricature of an interior *decorator*, not an interior designer.

Interior designers are actually more like architects than decorators. In fact, most have architectural training but have chosen to specialize in interiors. They are just as concerned with how well a floor is installed as with the colors of the floor itself. They can provide complete plans and specifications for any cosmetic face-lift project from the conversion of an attic into an office to the modernizing of a kitchen. They are qualified to provide advice and guidance on areas such as room layout, furnishings, fixtures, cabinets, lighting, flooring materials, wall and ceiling finishes, and all construction that isn't related to the home's structure or systems.

As with architects, the best place to turn for recommendations are other homeowners from the same socioeconomic group. You won't need to run your list of candidates by the local building department, since these plans won't need to be filed, but if you own a condominium or cooperative it does make sense to ask for the building board's or managing agent's opinion.

The interview of interior design candidates is similar to the interview of architects. It's very important to ask each candidate what percentage of their practice involves residential work, and what percentage of that involves renovations, since many interior designers specialize in commercial projects. You don't want to have your new family room end up looking like a doctor's waiting room. Ask if the designer has experience with your style of home. And obviously ask about fees and what services go along with them. Interior designers usually charge anywhere from $35 to $150 per hour. This fee includes job supervision and a full set of plans and specifications. Insist that a fee ceiling be established.

As with architects, it's important to make clear to the candidate interior designers that you have a budget in mind and intend to stick to it. If a candidate seems uncomfortable working within your budgetary limits end the interview immediately and move on to the next name.

The choice of an interior designer is a subjective one. While there are objective, structural, and mechanical elements to architectural work, most interior design is subjective and aesthetic. That's why it's especially important you and the designer see eye-to-eye on matters of taste. Again, avoid "name" people. You will be paying a premium and you'll be getting their taste, nor your own.

If your renovation project involves solely the cosmetic face-lift of a kitchen or bathroom you may want to consider hiring a specialized kitchen or bathroom planner. While not schooled in interior design, these individuals, commonly called space planners, are certified by the National Kitchen and Bathroom Association, and are trained in the products and principles of bathroom and kitchen design.

It can be difficult to find independent space planners—most are either employed by, or affiliated with, retailers who sell kitchen and bathroom appliances, cabinets, and fixtures—but if you can obtain one or two recommendations by all means interview them along with the interior designer candidates.

I don't recommend you use the on-staff planners at home centers for three reasons. First, you won't be selecting a designer, you'll be assigned one. Second, the plans will be tailored around the product and material lines that this particular home center carries and wants most to sell.

And third, the cost of the plans will be tied to the purchase of products and services from the home center. If you opt not to buy from this particular retailer or use their contracting service, but wish to keep the plans, you may end up spending more than you anticipated.

Independent planners generally charge from $35 to $50 per hour. One important difference between space planners and interior designers is that the former don't offer job supervision. If you do commission plans from an independent space planner you'll need to hire someone else to check up on the general contractor.

HOME INSPECTORS

People don't traditionally think of home inspectors when it comes time to renovate. But actually, they can be an invaluable part of your team. Think about it. Who better to come up with plans and specifications for system upgrades than an individual trained to spot problems in those systems? And who better to check up on work in progress and its completion than someone trained to spot shoddy workmanship? An experienced home inspector knows what products work best, and what's required for workmanship to stand up over a long period of time.

The best place to obtain recommendations for home inspectors is from a local real estate broker. Telephone the broker you used earlier to determine the effect your proposed renovation would have on your home's salability and ask them for recommendations. Since almost anyone can call themselves a home inspector, insist that the candidates be members of the American Society of Home Inspectors. You are looking for someone with a reputation for thoroughness and experience. Place the priority on experience. I'd rather push a ninety-year-old inspector around the project in a wheelchair than rely on a spry, but inexperienced, individual.

Explain to each candidate home inspector that you're considering a renovation project that doesn't involve design work (either a systems upgrade or a luxury addition), and you're looking for a home inspector who could prepare a list of specifications and provide some job supervision. Tell them that this list of specifications need not be a complex, formal document—it could even be handwritten. A simple narrative listing of the type and nature of materials that should be used and how they should be installed is sufficient for most jobs. For example: If you're having a new roof put on your house, you would need the inspector to note whether or not previous layers of shingles should be removed; what type of shingle should be installed and how; and what other incidental repairs should be made to the roof. The job supervision would entail two or three visits to the site: one or two while work is in progress and a final visit when work has been completed, to insure that the work is done according to the specifications.

Home inspectors usually charge between $100 and $300 per inspection. But for the type of work you're requesting—a list of specs, periodic visits to the site, and a final review—expect to pay anywhere from $500 to $1,000, or two percent of the total cost of the job. If you hired a space planner to prepare your kitchen or bathroom plans, and are hiring a home inspector to provide job supervision, expect to pay between $100 and $150 per visit.

Whichever professional you use to draft your plans and specifications and provide job supervision you'll need to formalize your relationship in an equitable, enforceable contract.

Your Contract With the Planning and Supervisory Professional

Most architects and designers use the American Institute of Architects standard form contract between a homeowner and design professional. But just because it is a form contract doesn't mean that changes can't be made. In fact, even though the standard form is surprisingly evenhanded, it's important to make sure certain things are included. The architect or designer may tell you not to worry about the language of the form, and say it's just a formality, but it's a legally binding, formal definition of your relationship and should be treated seriously. My advice is to have your attorney read and amend the contract. It should take her no more than two hours and cost you anywhere from $150 to $500, depending on her hourly fee.

The contract should state explicitly the responsibilities of the architect or designer. Fees, payment schedules, and ownership of the plans and drawings are all negotiable and should also be described fully. Since architects and interior designers view projects in terms of stages—designing, drafting plans, bidding, construction—it often works out best if you pay them a set amount after completion of each stage. This insures that, if you break the relationship or decide not to follow through on the project, you haven't paid for more services than you have actually received. Make sure that the terms under which the architect or interior designer are entitled to their fees are clearly stated. For example: The fee for the drafting of plans should not be due until the plans have met your approval. A clause should be included that describes how your relationship with the architect or designer can be terminated and what happens to the plans and drawings if it is.

Perhaps the most important section of the contract is the area where the scope of services is spelled out. Regardless of what the architect or interior designer says to you, he or she is not required to do anything that isn't specifically mentioned in the contract. If you expect the architect to provide you with a model as well as three sets of blueprints it should be stated in the contract. If you want the interior designer to show up three times to check on the progress of the job, and then make a final inspection, the contract must state exactly that.

Independent space planners sometimes also use the AIA form, or they have a custom form drafted for them. Make sure that the same important clauses mentioned above are amended or added to the space planner's contract.

Rather than resort to a formal contract with a home inspector, you should ask your lawyer to write up a simple letter contract that outlines the terms of the arrangement and the payment schedule. I'd advise you to pay in stages when the work has been done. For example: If you agree that for a fee of $500 the home inspector will draw up a list of specs, visit the site three times while the job is underway, and then make a final inspection when the work is completed, I'd arrange to pay out $100 upon receipt of the specs, $100 after each inspection, and $100 after the final review ($100 × 5 = $500). It should take your lawyer less than a hour to draft this type of agreement.

Construction managers usually have their own custom contracts. Since their services are only required in substantial, expensive projects, it would be foolish not to have your attorney spend an hour going over the contract, adding to it and amending it as necessary. When you're talking about construction costs of over $100,000, architectural fees of more than $13,000, and supervisory fees of around

$2,000, spending another $150 to $250 to insure that you are fully protected makes sense.

Working With Your Planning Professional

Now that you've contracted with someone to draft your plans and specifications and supervise the job, it's time to work with them. Even the simple spec sheet your home inspector prepares needs to be discussed. It's not enough to tell the inspector you want a "good" roof. Good is a relative term. There are roofs built to last ten years and roofs built to last thirty years. Both are good if they live up to expectations. As you may imagine, a thirty-year roof will cost more than a ten-year roof. If you can see yourself moving within ten years, it may not make sense to invest in a thirty-year roof. You and the inspector need to sit down and discuss exactly what you're looking for, and how much you're willing, or able, to spend.

While that conversation may take only an hour or so, planning a remodeling project, space addition, or cosmetic face-lift can take a lot longer. Don't expect to sit down with an architect or interior designer for an hour, explaining what you would like, and then receive a perfect set of plans in a couple of days. This is a process of give and take that can take anywhere from a couple of weeks to six months, depending on the complexity of the project.

Don't let the time involved trouble you. It's actually beneficial. One of the advantages of having a comprehensive set of plans is that it minimizes the potential for surprises and added charges once the job begins. Residential construction projects have a tendency to grow once they've gotten underway. Your kitchen is half demolished, and you're already spending $10,000, so you ask yourself, "Why not change the window and add some skylights?" Renovations are so complex, expensive, and disruptive, that while they're going on most people say they'll never go through it again. They try to squeeze everything they can into the job once it's begun, in an effort to get more out of it.

The problem with this approach is that having the general contractor do something not originally in the plans (called a "change order" in the trade) can be very expensive. It may cost you fifteen dollars for each electrical outlet specified in the plan—but fifty dollars for each you add afterwards. This surcharge is a not so subtle attempt by the general contractor and/or the electrician to cash in on spur of the moment inspirations.

Rather than stifle your urge to get the most for your money, or swallow a huge change order bill, why not spend time studying the plan, and thinking about it, before submitting it for bids. I suggest that after you and your family get a set of plans you like, you live with them for at least a month. If you think it will help, pay the extra money for a model or a set of three-dimensional interior drawings.

Try to envision yourself in the house after the renovations have been done. Will you be happy? Is there anything you'll miss? Have you forgotten anything? Pay particular attention to electrical outlets, telephone jacks, cable TV plugs, and storage space. Think about all of the things you do during the course of the day. Where will you do them? Where will the laundry be folded? Where will you store the vacuum cleaner and household cleaning supplies? Where will the lawn furniture go during the winter? The longer you spend studying, considering, and just plain looking at your plans, the more likely they'll be complete and the less likely you'll be to want expensive additions once the project has started.

Try to be as specific as possible when going over

sketches and draft plans with the architect or interior designer. Don't worry about hurting their feelings—their job is to get inside your head and put that design on the paper. While specificity helps, don't be afraid to offer abstract criticisms, such as a feeling that a room is "too heavy". Architects and interior designers know what concrete elements contribute to these abstract impressions and can adjust plans accordingly.

Be wary of architects or interior designers who, once the job is underway, will try to increase the scope of a proposed renovation project. Two clients of mine—a married couple who are both successful actors—hired an architect to draw up plans for a renovation of their New England farm. It wasn't a major job, but it did involve changes to the facade of their home, so architectural plans were needed. After a couple of months they came to me and said they were having problems keeping the architect from going overboard. I decided to visit with the architect to see if I could help. When I explained the limited scope of the project, the architect balked. "I'm not a hired pencil," he said, adding, "I have to get into their heads." What he should have said was, "I want to get into their wallets." Knowing money was no obstacle to these clients, he continued to try to convince them they actually needed a major renovation. Needless to say they severed their relationship with him and found someone else willing to draft plans for the limited renovation they wanted.

Once you've lived with the plans and are sure they address your needs and wants it's time to find people capable of turning the piece of paper into reality.

CHAPTER 6

Selecting General Contractor Candidates

───

Surround yourself with the highest caliber people. Remember that first-rate people hire first-rate people—while second-rate people hire third-rate people.
—RICHARD M. WHITE, JR.

After living with the plans and specifications for a while, and hammering out the design details, you'll probably be eager to get the job underway. Don't get too excited. There's still quite a bit left to do, and it requires a level head.

Selecting a general contractor isn't simply a matter of soliciting bids from a handful of candidates and then choosing the low bidder—or at least it shouldn't be. Anyone can call themselves a general contractor. That makes the selection of a general contractor for your job a studied, time-consuming process. It's actually made up of five distinct steps. First, you must determine what type of general contractor is right for the job. Second, you must find at least three qualified candidates. Third, you must carefully investigate the craftsmanship, character, and financial stability of each candidate. Fourth, you must scrupulously analyze each bid. And finally, you must negotiate an airtight contract with the general contractor you select for the job. Rushing the selection of a general contractor is a recipe for disappointment: According to one recent national survey, only 20 percent of all homeowners were totally satisfied with the job their general contractors did. Now that I've cooled your ardor a bit, let's examine each step.

GENERALISTS VERSUS SPECIALISTS

General contractors fall into two major categories: traditional general contractors and specialists. The traditional general contractor is able, or at least claims to be able, to do any type of work. Whether you're looking to finish a basement, redo a kitchen, or expand dormers into rooms, a generalist should be able to marshal and coordinate the trades. His or her experience will be broad-based. A specialist general contractor is, like a medical specialist, someone who concentrates on one particular type of project. You can find general contractors who specialize in almost every popular renovation. While they too marshal and coordinate trades, their primary experience will be in their area of specialization.

Initially the choice may seem obvious: Go for the specialist. However, that presupposes your renovation will be clearly defined. If all you're looking for is someone to build a deck, then yes, it makes sense to turn to a general contractor who specializes in building decks. But if, for example, you're adding a deck and also having a kitchen face-lift done, you'll need to look for a generalist. Try to break your project down into subprojects. If it separates easily, you need a generalist. If it's impossible to subdivide you need a specialist.

Making the right choice is very important. If you select two generalists and one specialist to bid on a specialized project you're setting yourself up for trouble. Take the case of John and Beth Greyhare, the couple who are transforming the former family homestead into the retirement home of their dreams. They've decided that they will break the process down into a series of separate smaller projects. The first step is to add a raised deck, with sliding glass doors leading from the dining room, to the rear of their house.

The Greyhares call in two generalists whose names they got from friends, and one specialist recommended by a nearby nursery to bid on the deck project. The two generalists, unsure of the potential problems, underbid the job. The specialist, well aware of what could go wrong, comes in substantially higher. Even though the Greyhares have gone through the trouble of having comprehensive plans and specs drawn up, they're still getting bids that are apples and oranges. And human nature being what it is, they select one of the two lower bids.

As the job progresses and unforeseen problems crop up, the general contractor complains about losing money on the project. John holds up the signed contract with a budget price and, as nicely as possible, tells him that if he's losing money it's his own fault. The general contractor realizes he has no recourse but takes it out on the job. It isn't intentional; when a general contractor and his subcontractors feel they're losing money, they unconsciously throw craftsmanship out the sliding glass doors they're installing and work as quickly as possible. By soliciting, and then selecting, a bid from the wrong type of general contractor, the Greyhares will get exactly what they paid for: a substandard job.

SELECTING THE RIGHT GENERALISTS

If you've determined a generalist is what you need, things will get even more complicated. There are actually three different types of generalists. The general contractor who has an office downtown, with architects, designers, carpenters, and masons on staff, and who builds million-dollar homes, is very different from the general contractor who works from his home, is on site every day supervising the subcontractors, and who does mainly renovations. And they're both a far cry from the general contractor who does his own carpentry and whose office is the cab of his pickup truck. The first may never submit his bids much less than $100,000, because his overhead demands a certain amount of revenue. The second probably won't take on jobs at either end of the scale. Smaller projects aren't worth her time, and larger ones may be beyond her means. The third certainly couldn't handle a major project, and may not be able to afford to do a midsized job, but would be very comfortable taking on a small one. I've simplified matters somewhat, since general contractors don't fit into three well-defined categories. But for the sake of your sanity, assume the selection of a generalist general contractor is like the old story "Goldilocks and the Three Bears": one is too big, one is too small, and one is just right. The trick is figuring out which size is just right for you.

Once again, selecting the wrong size generalist can be disastrous. That's because, being in business to make money, general contractors will look at your project in a couple of different ways. They'll calculate how much it will cost them, and then they'll decide how much they want the work.

Let's go back to Michael and Barbara Newparent, the young couple who are adding onto their home. They asked three different size generalists to bid on the job, which they and their architect budgeted at $50,000. The larger general contractor calculated the job would actually cost $50,000 including his profit, but since he doesn't like to do jobs for less than $100,000, and didn't want to tie up his crew for small potatoes, presented the Newparents with a bid for $85,000. If they went for it, fine, he'd pocket the added profit. If they didn't, he'd just find another job. The smaller general contractor also figures the Newparents' project would cost $50,000. But he was desperate for work and eager to start doing bigger jobs—after all, that's how little general contractors become big general contractors. He decided to cut his profit and gamble there would be no unforeseen problems. He handed the Newparents a bid for $35,000. The midsized general contractor, who had the most experience on similar jobs, came up with a price of $50,000, but since the Newparents were asking for a budget price, added a cushion of $10,000, result in a bid of $60,000.

The Newparents now had three bids of $35,000, $60,000, and $85,000 for a job they figured would cost about $50,000. They'd be crazy to accept the high bid. The greedy part of them wanted to tell the higher bidder to drop dead, thank the middle bidder for her time, and grab the bid for $35,000. But in their hearts they knew something had gone wrong. It had. They had limited their choices dramatically by going to the wrong size general contractors. They've really only obtained a single bid—the one for $60,000. The other two are worthless. Now they've no idea whether or not $60,000 is actually a competitive price. If they had instead gone to three midsized general contractors they might have obtained bids of $55,000, $60,000, and $65,000. Then they could have selected the general contractor who seemed the most experienced, skilled, and financially solvent.

It's essential, therefore, to get all your bids from the right size general contractors. You can't count on them to tell you a job is too big or too small. Since no businessperson passes up a chance to make money, general contractors will bid on every job. It's up to you to determine who's right for your job.

Finding the Right Candidates

The best way to develop a list of general contractor candidates who are both the right size and the right type for your job is to get some expert advice. Going to friends and neighbors won't work since they've no idea of how to match general contractors up with projects. Just because they used Sumien Construction to build their deck, and it's still standing, doesn't mean you should. They may have overpaid, gotten less than satisfactory workmanship, or just lucked out. You also shouldn't rely on recommendations from lumberyards, home centers, or paint stores—they'll just give you the names of their customers. Go instead to knowledgeable unbiased sources: your architect, designer, construction manager, space planner, and/or home inspector.

Stress that you're looking for the right general contractor for the job, not the cheapest. It can be a real advantage if your design professional has a good working relationship with the general contractor you select—the job can become a team project rather than a battle of wills or egos in which you'll be the only loser. But there's also a danger. Since you'll be relying on your design or supervisory professional to act as a watchdog on the general contractor, you don't want them to be too close. If the general contractor on your job just happens to be the architect's golfing buddy, your watchdog could turn into a rubber stamp. That's why I'd also run the recommended names past the local building department, a member of the coop board or homeowners' association, or a representative of the managing agent. Using a general contractor okayed by a bureaucracy you'll need to deal with later on could be an added insurance policy against any potential problems.

Buy yourself three file folders—one for each general contractor—and place a complete set of plans and specifications in each. Telephone the general contractors, explain who you are, on whose recommendations you're calling, and what you're calling about. Finally, schedule an appointment for them to stop by your house.

MEETING WITH THE CANDIDATES

It's important to develop the correct attitude toward your meetings with general contractor candidates. Don't let them use this as an opportunity to sell you. Instead, make sure you control the agenda and flow of the meeting. Some general contractors are more salesmen than craftsmen; some are so slick and spellbinding they could sell the Brooklyn Bridge to former New York City mayor Ed Koch. Take charge of the meeting from the first moment.

When each general contractor arrives, hand him a copy of your plans and specifications. It's perfectly alright, and in fact, probably beneficial, if the general contractor sees you have another two folders next to his own. Competition is healthy. Explain that you're looking for a budget price. Some general contractors will object to doing business this way, and will instead offer to come up with a price based on time and materials. This gives them a great deal more latitude, and insures they at least won't lose money on the job. Unfortunately, it also invariably leads to both time and cost overruns. Asking for a budget price puts a great deal of pressure on the general contractor to come up with accurate cost estimates. That's tough to do since in renovations there could always be unforeseen problems. But in providing them with comprehensive plans you've made their job considerably easier. To insure they'll be covered in any eventuality, the general contractors will probably bump their price up from 10 to 20 percent. You can help offset this surcharge, and perhaps overcome their reticence, by offering bonuses if the job comes in under budget and ahead of schedule. For example, offer to split any cost savings equally with the general contractor. However, you'll also want to add penalties for delays.

Never give any hint as to what your proposed budget is. If you let the general contractors know you've been working with the idea of spending $50,000, none will come in with a bid of less, even if they could.

Ask for the bids to be broken down by individual trades. You're going to want to be able to spot any problems with the subcontractors prior to commissioning the job. A general contractor may have two or three electricians she uses regularly. She may select the one she likes best, but who also is the most expensive. You want the opportunity to be able to ask the general contractor to go back and get a price from another, less expensive subcontractor.

In addition, ask them to include information on how much they'll charge for extras, such as adding another light switch or electrical outlet. A general contractor can charge for extras in a couple of ways. If the extras are added before the work is actually begun, the general contractor could simply pass along the standard charge. However, he might want to add a penalty charge to discourage you from adding anything to the plans, just as he would if you wanted a change made once work had begun. It's better to broach this issue now, at the bidding stage, since you still have leverage over the general contractor—he presumably wants the job. Once you've made a choice, the general contractor has all the leverage and is under no pressure to be reasonable. His prices jump from wholesale to retail levels.

Explain that even though you want them to bid on the plans and specifications, you don't want to stifle them. If they've suggestions that could somehow improve the project aesthetically they should list them separately and indicate the effect they'd have on the bottom line. Similarly, ask them to take note of any places where they think you can save money by altering the plans. Finally, ask them to indicate if they find any gaps or mistakes in the plans and how they should be corrected. Just make sure the general contractors understand their suggestions and corrections must be listed separately from the rest of the bid, so that you're able to compare bids.

Savvy general contractors may be able to save you a great deal of money. Architects and designers often fall in love with new or very expensive materials, not realizing, or caring, that there are less expensive alternatives. On one project I was involved in the architect specified redwood siding for a pool house. Redwood would indeed have looked wonderful, and may well have lasted for a century. But it would also have cost a small fortune. The general contractor came to me and said that if we used cedar siding stained to look like redwood, it would cut the cost in half. Granted, it would probably last fifty, not one hundred years, but this was a home, not a monument. When I asked the architect about it, he readily agreed. He hadn't realized there was such a difference between the costs of the two woods.

Ask general contractors for the names of three jobs they've done that are the most like yours, so you can see a relevant example of their workmanship. And, if possible, get jobs that span at least the past three years so you can judge how well the work has held up. (The ideal list would be a one-year-old project, a two-year-old project, and a three-year-old project.) The general contractors may not have this information with them, or on the top of their heads, so give them a couple of days to come up with it—but insist they do. (Beware of any general contractor who discourages you from visiting their previous jobs and instead offers just photos as evidence of their work.)

Ask each general contractor to provide you with a bank reference and a business reference also (preferably one of their suppliers), and to include a copy of their credit file in their bidding package. If any candidate refuses to provide this information, he or she has something to hide and should be scratched off your list. (For a checklist of all the things to ask candidate general contractors during this meeting see page 130.)

While the general contractors are busy deciphering the plans, soliciting prices from their subcontractors, and preparing their bids, you'll be busy investigating them. That's because bids can only tell you what the job will cost, not whether it will be done well, or on time.

INVESTIGATING CANDIDATES

As soon as the general contractor candidates leave your home, pick up the telephone and call the local chapter of the Better Business Bureau. Ask the representative handling your call if they've any information—positive or negative—about your three general contractor candidates. Contact the nearest office of your state's department of consumer affairs or consumer protection agency and repeat the request. Record all the information you receive in the relevant file. Don't be surprised if there are a couple of complaints on file. Almost every business person, whether honest or corrupt, has run-ins with customers. Try to get information about the complaints so you can ask the general contractors about them later on—that will demonstrate you're not to be taken lightly. Find out if the number of complaints is more, less, or just about average for the trade.

Next, contact your attorney and ask him to find out if there are any liens or judgments against the candidate contractors. He should be able to do this for a fee of from $75 to $100. If yours is a sizable project ask your attorney to obtain a Dun & Bradstreet report on each general contractor. This will cost anywhere from $300 to $600.

Telephone the bank and business references given by the general contractors. Explain who you are and simply say that you're looking to make sure the contractor in question is both reliable and financially solvent. If you approach the matter without too much undue formality you'll be surprised at how forthcoming people will be with information. (For a list of all the steps involved in investigating general contractors see page 130.)

While you're running around stop by your insurance broker's office. Explain what type of work you're going to have done, and ask the broker to make a judgment of your potential exposure and whether or not you're adequately protected by your homeowner's policy. Tell the broker that if she finds you need more protection, you'd like some price quotes for a sufficient temporary rider to your home-owner's coverage.

INTERVIEWING REFERENCES

By this time you should have gotten references from all of the general contractor candidates. Write their names and addresses on separate sheets of paper and add them to your files. Make it your business to call each reference and schedule an appointment. Yes, I know that means making nine visits. But each shouldn't take more than fifteen minutes, and there's no other way to get an accurate measurement of the quality of a general contractor's service and craftsmanship. At each reference you'll simultaneously be looking for signs of the skill and professionalism of the subcontractors used, and quizzing the homeowner about what it was like working with the general contractor. The next chapter covers the signs of good workmanship for every trade. For now, let's concentrate on what you should be asking the homeowner about the general contractor.

By asking for only comparable projects, and specifying that they come from a three-year period, you minimize the degree to which the general contractor can set you up with shills. Still, you wouldn't have the names of these people if the general contractor thought they'd give a less than glowing endorsement. For that reason you must be very deliberate in your questioning. You're not interested in eliciting opinions, only facts. Rather than asking subjective questions like, what did you think of his work?, you should ask objective questions such as, did he personally come to the house every day that his crew was here? In other words, ask only yes or no questions: Did the project go over budget? did it take longer than was planned? was the general contractor there everyday? were the workers polite? did they clean up at the end of each day? did the general contractor come back to take care of mistakes? has the project needed to be repaired since it was completed? does the skylight leak? are the windows and doors drafty?

Don't be embarrassed to bring a list of questions with you on the visits. (I've included the beginnings of such a list on page 131.) Consider attaching it to the back of a clipboard and using the front to hold your notes for this particular visit. You're probably never going to see this person again, so if they think you're neurotic and nosy, who cares? Anyway, when it comes to hiring a general contractor, it's better to be neurotic and nosy than laid-back and unconcerned.

While you're speaking to the homeowners who have used your candidate general contractors, you're also going to be looking around for signs of how good a job was done. For an idea of what those signs are, turn to the next chapter.

When you return home from each visit to a reference job, place your notes on craftsmanship and the homeowners' responses to your questions about the general contractor in the proper file. By the time you finish making all nine visits you'll probably receive calls from the general contractors saying they've finished their bids and will be dropping them off. Most will want to drop off the bids in person. That gives them a chance to explain their calculations and to try to sell you. Agree to a visit, listen attentively to what each has to say, take notes if necessary, but remain noncommittal. Don't let them pressure you into making a decision right there. Thank them politely for their efforts, and explain you'll be getting back to them after you and your design professional have had a chance to look the bids over.

CHECKLIST FOR INTERVIEWING GENERAL CONTRACTORS

The following is a list of the questions to ask, information to obtain from, and points to explain to each candidate general contractor during your initial meeting.

1. a budget, or fixed price for the job, as specifically defined by the plans
2. a bid broken down by trades
3. a list of the costs of potential extras, such as adding another light switch, electrical outlet, etc.
4. any suggestions they have to improve the project
5. any suggestions they have to cut the cost of the project
6. any gaps or mistakes in the plans
7. the names of three jobs they have worked on, similar to your proposed project, stretching back up to three years ago
8. a bank reference
9. a business reference
10. a copy of their personal credit file

CHECKLIST FOR INVESTIGATING GENERAL CONTRACTORS

While candidate general contractors are preparing their bids, you should be investigating their financial solvency and business ethics. The steps involved in this investigation are:

1. contact the local Better Business Bureau
2. contact the local department of consumer affairs or consumer protection agency
3. have your attorney do a lien and judgment search, and if appropriate, obtain Dun & Bradstreet reports
4. contact the general contractor's banking reference

5. contact the general contractor's business reference

CHECKLIST OF QUESTIONS TO ASK HOMEOWNER REFERENCES

The following is a list of general questions to ask home-owners given as references by candidate general contractors.

1. did the project begin on schedule?
2. did the general contractor show up at least once a day?
3. was the crew punctual?
4. did the crew clean up at the end of the day?
5. did the crew take excessive breaks during the day?
6. did the crew work up until 5:00 P.M. every day?
7. did you have any problems with the building department?
8. did the job come in on schedule and within the budget?
9. did you have any problems after the job was "finished"?
10. did the general contractor come back to resolve problems?

These general questions should be supplemented by more specific questions dealing with the type of project you are contemplating. For example: If the job involves skylights an important question would be: Do the skylights leak? Remember, questions should always be phrased to elicit a yes or no answer.

CHAPTER 7

Judging Subcontractors' Work

———

Criticism comes easier than craftsmanship.

—ZEUXIS

You might be surprised to find a chapter with this title in a book that advocates the almost universal use of general contractors. After all, one advantage of using a general contractor is that you won't need to go out and find individual tradespeople. Still, it's important to have some understanding of how to judge the work of various trades. To a large degree you'll be judging general contractors by the quality of the subcontractors they use. That's because much of what general contractors do themselves is invisible. There's no telltale sign of how well a job was managed other than that it came in close to schedule and budget. The only way to find that out is to speak to previous customers. But you can often judge the quality of subcontractors simply by looking around.

There are also times when you'll need to hire subcontractors directly. If your kitchen faucet leaks or you must replace the light fixture in the bathroom, even I don't recommend you call in a general contractor. Instead you should find a plumber or electrician on your own. And as long as I'm going to provide you with a list of the signs of professionalism for individual trades and tips on finding them, I thought I might as well include information on trades general contractors rarely use but homeowners often need. (For an idea of the hourly fees for various trades see the chart at the end of this chapter. For an idea of project costs refer back to the charts at the end of chapter 2.)

AWNING AND CANOPY INSTALLERS

These tradespeople work directly with retailers or product manufacturers and are usually referred through the place of purchase. Since they come as a package, when visiting homes where previous work was done you'll need to check on both the product and the installation. Any problems with framing or mounting hardware can generally be traced to the installation; problems with the canvas itself should be blamed on the manufacturer. Guarantees from installers are only as good as the health of their business, so only deal with established firms.

BASEMENT WATERPROOFERS

Since this trade has more than its share of incompetents and con artists it's important to be doubly careful and always check with the Better Business Bureau. One problem with even legitimate waterproofing contractors is that most specialize in one particular type of process and advocate their specialty whether or not it's the best option in your case. That's why it makes sense to first hire a home inspector to diagnose the cause of the problem and recommend a treatment, and then to solicit contractors for that specific treatment. A basement water problem may actually be caused by faulty leaders and gutters or poor site drainage. The sign of good workmanship in a waterproofing contractor is simple: Contact previous customers who had the same problem as yours and ask them if it has been eliminated.

CABINET REFACERS AND REFINISHERS

Homeowners in search of an inexpensive kitchen face-lift often turn to these specialists. Refinishing means stripping the old stain or paint off the cabinets and restaining or repainting. Refacing means replacing or adding a layer of veneer directly on top of the existing finish. It's tough to generalize about the cost of these projects, but the accepted rule of thumb is that refinishing costs two thirds, and refacing costs one half of the price of entirely new cabinetry. Since you don't know what the cabinets looked like before you can't rely on a visual inspection of a previous job to get an accurate reading on their skill. Most pros, however, will have a book containing before and after photos for you to look through. If they don't have such a book they're either rookies or have something to hide. A kitchen design store may be willing to provide some recommendations as long as you're buying other items from them.

CARPENTERS

When you think of home renovation the image that comes to mind is of a carpenter banging nails. The reason is that the majority of work done on most projects is carpentry. That also accounts for why most general contractors begin as carpenters. Generally, if it doesn't involve wires, pipes, or stone, it's the carpenter's job. That doesn't mean all carpenters are generalists. In fact, if you browse through this chapter you'll find that many of the specialized trades are actually offshoots of carpentry. Aside from these specialties there are two major types of carpentry—framing and finishing.

Framing is the rough carpentry work of building everything up from the foundation wall, including exterior and interior wall framing, exterior wall sheathing, roof rafters, and roof sheathing. The framing crew will also install all exterior doors and windows, and construct such outside details as soffits, fascias, and rakes. Finishing consists of detail work such as building cabinets and installing interior window trim, interior doors and trim, and moldings.

While most carpenters will claim they can do both framing and finishing, larger crews employ specialists. The framing carpenters will usually be younger with broad biceps. The finish carpenter will have a touch of grey in his hair, and probably be wearing glasses from repeatedly checking all those minute measurements. The best place to turn for the names of potential carpenters is to other homeowners who have had similar work done.

It's tough to make a judgment on framing work since none of it is visible after a job has been completed. But if you are lucky enough to see a framing crew at work on another job, there are some things to look for. The sills—the wood that sits on the foundation walls—should be pressure-treated lumber. There should be a continuous sill sealer—½-inch thick fiberglass or foam insulation the same width as the sill—between the wood and the foundation wall. While 2″ × 4″ framing is acceptable, most work today is done with 2″ × 6″s. That's to provide room for another two inches of insulation, not for added strength. So if you are having work done in an area with extreme temperatures 2″ × 6″s are preferable. All framing should be sixteen inches on center. In other words there should be no more than sixteen inches from the center of one stud to the next. Real pros will use pneumatic nail guns to speed up the job. An added bonus for the homeowner is that the nails used in these guns are coated with resin or glue, making them less likely to pull out. Check to see if studs are "toe-nailed." That means nails have been driven diagonally through the end of the studs and joists into the plate or beam. While "toe nailing" is required by most codes, inspectors often overlook it, and some framers try to cheat on it to save time and money. Floor joists should be at least 2″ × 10″s, also sixteen inches on center. Especially long spans, however, may require 2″ × 12″s or some form of specially engineered joist. Subflooring should be either ¾-inch thick tongue and groove plywood or two layers of at least ½-inch-thick plywood. The plywood should be installed perpendicular to the floor joists, and the seams should be staggered.

Finish carpentry is easier to examine. Look for neat, clean cuts and tight joints. You shouldn't see any saw or hammer marks. The margins between doors and their frames should be even all around. Pay extra attention to the corner joints of moldings. A good carpenter will make sure there's no visible gap. Cabinets should be screwed into the wall, not nailed. Real pros will use pneumatic or electric screwdrivers. When having skylights installed, check previous jobs with skylights and ask the magic question: "Do they leak?"

CARPET INSTALLERS

Most carpet installers are hired through carpet retailers, and while there's a great deal of turnover in the business, there are some real pros around. Fees usually run around three to five dollars a square yard, and six dollars per step. There's usually an additional charge if the carpet needs to be worked around the balusters. Be prepared to buy more carpeting than you may think was necessary. First, not all carpet comes in 12-foot wide rolls. Second, all carpets have a grain or direction in which the goods were woven. To have a flawless job done you may need to buy as much as 25 to 50 percent more carpet than the actual square footage of the room.

It's fairly easy to spot a quality carpet installation. Check around walls and doorjambs, looking to see that the carpet is flat rather than bunched up. Patterns should be parallel to the most visible adjacent wall. A professional spends as much time preparing as installing; places padding under carpets; and locates seams in unobtrusive areas. In fact, if you can easily spot a seam the job wasn't done well. Pros use tackless strips (lengths of wood with small nails sticking out of them) around the edges of a room, make seams with a special tape and heat iron, and use "knee kickers" (a tubular device which has at one end a claw to grip the carpet, and at the other a pad which is kicked with the installer's knee) to stretch the carpet tight.

CEILING INSTALLERS

Suspended and acoustical tile ceiling are popular additions, particularly in finished basements. While any good carpenter should be able to install a ceiling, there are specialists who work through the stores that sell ceiling kits. The signs of professionalism are the edge rows of panels—they should all be at least half a tile—and how well obstacles are concealed. A real pro will visit the site before giving an estimate.

CENTRAL AUDIO/VIDEO SYSTEM INSTALLERS

The compact disc player and the video cassette recorder have sparked a renewed interest in home entertainment electronics. However, many homeowners don't like the idea of turning the audio/video system into the focus of their interiors—a sort of high tech hearth. In response, specialized contractors able to install centralized, hidden systems, have sprung up. The best sources for names are local high-end audio salons. The prices of these systems depend on their size and scope and the quality of the individual components. Try to deal with a company that uses off-the-shelf components rather than proprietary equipment. This will allow you to check their prices against other sources and separate out their installation charges. One telltale sign of skill is how well wiring is hidden.

CHIMNEY SWEEPS

This is one of those trades that, for whatever reason, tends to attract free spirits. But sweeping chimneys is serious business. The soot and creosote that builds up in fireplaces and wood stoves can become a huge fire hazard and should be cleaned at least once a year. Many chimney sweeps also do maintenance work on wood stoves, chimneys, and fireplaces. They generally charge a flat fee to clean a stove or fireplace, but bill hourly for other jobs. The secret is to find someone who has been in the business for a long time.

DECK BUILDERS

One excellent way for young framing carpenters to become full-fledged general contractors is to specialize in building decks. Most of the job is framing, and the work required by other trades is fairly minimal: An excavator might be needed to dig holes for the posts; a mason may be needed to pour the footings; an electrician could be called in to move outlets or add exterior lighting; and a house painter may be needed to touch up if a sliding glass door had to be added. Outdoor furniture stores and nurseries are two good sources for names. Ask candidates for reference jobs more than two years old so you can see how well they've held up.

Once you've found an older job, check if boards are still straight, nail heads are still flush, and there are no split ends. There should also be no rough edges that could cause splinters on railings or benches. Other signs of professionalism are found around the ledger—that's the board installed against the house to which all the joists are then attached. Pros will have removed the siding and then bolted the ledger directly to the structural framing through the exterior sheathing. Flashing should be installed around the ledger to prevent moisture from getting to the sheathing. The original siding should then have been reinstalled to fit neatly around the ledger. The joists should be attached to the ledger using U-shaped galvanized steel connectors (they are called Tico Hangers) and should be spaced no more than sixteen inches on center. The boards themselves should be no more than one quarter to three eighths of an inch apart. (When installed they should be no more than one eighth of an inch apart, but over time they will shrink anywhere from one eighth to one quarter inch in width.) Stairs should be at least thirty-six inches wide and 2-inch stock should have been used for the treads. Railings should be at least thirty-six inches high with a maximum spacing between spindles of six inches.

When discussing your job with contractors be aware that "pressure treated" is a general term. Your plans should be more specific, stating that only chromated copper arsenate (CCA) treated lumber of at least number two grade be used throughout. If you want to use cedar or redwood, consider construction rather than clear grades— the cost savings could be substantial and there will be no fall off in water or insect resistance. While some deck builders advocate using premachined 1¼-inch decking because it has rounded edges, avoid it. While cost-effective for the contractor it is thinner and therefore more prone to cracking, splitting, and cupping than the traditional 2-inch stock. Insist that the concrete footings for your deck should extend below the frost line in your area. That means they should be at least thirty-six inches deep unless they're being poured on a rock ledge or in a sandy area not prone to freeze and thaw cycles.

These same contractors usually build outdoor play structures. Once again, check older jobs. Pay particular attention to: how well sanded the edges of the structure are; the height and location of handrails; the strength and security of ladders and climbing posts; and whether or not the hardware is recessed or countersunk.

DECK AND SIDING CLEANERS

There are very few full-time deck and siding cleaners. Most are members of a siding crew who have leased a power sprayer and gone into business on the side to pick up some extra dollars. That's why the best source for names is a siding or deck contractor. Because of their lack of accountability and professionalism it's very important to interview carefully and check references. Look for a knowledgeable individual. Ask about the toxicity of the detergent they'll be using, and whether it affects animals or plants. Find out if it contains a mildew retardant. Generally, hand washings cost more than power washings, but they won't accelerate the deterioration of older siding. Fees are usually based on a square-foot price.

DECORATIVE PAINTERS

A decorative painter is more artist than craftsperson. These individuals do custom paint finishes such as stenciling, marbelizing, sponging, and ragging. Most work strictly on referrals through architects, designers, or interior decorators, and charge two dollars per square foot and up. They won't be able to provide an accurate estimate until you and your design professional have selected a pattern and they've had a chance to see the site. Don't expect to get a chance to see their work in person. Most prefer to offer photographic evidence of prior jobs. In addition, be prepared to arrange for the prep work yourself. Decorative painters are understandably finicky about how the walls are to be prepared, but generally won't do the work required.

DRIVEWAY CONTRACTORS

There are three types of driveway contractors: those who build driveways, those who resurface driveways, and those who both build and resurface. I advise you to steer clear of contractors who only do resurfacing. That is one of the biggest rip-off businesses in America and the chances of getting taken are very high.

When installing or resurfacing an asphalt drive, stick with contractors who are members of the National Asphalt Pavement Association and who have been in business for more than five years. You can usually tell a professional from an amateur by the tools they use. The only time a professional will use a hand roller is to level out a small patch. Pros will also arrive in their own dump truck with a sizable crew. And even if an asphalt contractor looks, acts, and talks like a pro, check out their references carefully.

If you're having a concrete driveway built make sure you visit at least three older references to see how well they've aged. Look for driveways that are as straight and perpendicular to the roadway as possible. Check if the driveway is either pitched (higher on one side than the other) or crowned (higher in the middle than the edge) to allow for proper drainage. Every concrete drive should have asphalt expansion strips at least four inches wide that appear at least every twenty feet of its length. There should also be a final asphalt extension strip where the garage floor meets the driveway.

Drywall Installers

While most carpenters and painters will patch drywall (also known as gypsum wallboard, GWB, or Sheetrock), a major installation should only be done by a specialist. Since it's a volume business these contractors work in crews and aim for speed. Generally there are two types of crew members: those who hang the boards, called "Sheetrockers," and those who finish the seams, called "tapers." Since the job depends on accurate framing and preparation they're usually loathe to work directly for homeowners. Even though they move quickly, a good drywall team's work should result in seamless walls with clean, sharp corners, and no dimples or craters.

The best crews begin by sealing all openings and vents with plastic. The Sheetrockers should then use screws to install drywall that's at least ½-inch thick. (Thinner sheets may be used in special circumstances, such as when installing drywall directly over plaster walls.) They generally use sheets that are 4' × 8', though 6-, 10-, and 12-foot lengths are also available. While longer sheets lead to fewer seams, and therefore a smoother finish, the 10- and 12-foot lengths are more difficult to maneuver into place. The sheets should be installed perpendicular to the direction of the framing members. Butt joints—where two 4-foot edges meet—should be staggered. Outside corners should be finished with metal corner beads, which are nailed into place. The tapers will follow the Sheetrockers placing joint tape and three coats of spackle. Expert tapers will form joints approximately eight inches wide along the longer side of the sheet, and ten to twelve inches wide along the shorter side. That's because the long edges of Sheetrock are made with tapered edges while the shorter edges are not. The average charge for a drywall installation is twenty-five dollars per 4' × 8' sheet.

ELECTRICIANS

Electrical work is complex and potentially dangerous. That's why it's one of the most highly regulated fields. Electricians must be licensed by both the state and the local municipality, insured, and bonded. Since there's no way for you to check an electrician's work you'll need to rely on their references and affiliations. The electrician should be a member of the National Electrical Contractors Association and have been trained in a program sponsored by the International Brotherhood of Electrical Workers. There's a great deal of difference between doing electrical work in new construction and having to snake wires through old plaster walls, so make sure the electrician has the proper experience. It's okay to hire your own electrician when the work in question involves solely the electrical system: adding outlets, switches, or fixtures; running a new line for a major appliance; or updating service. If the work involves any other systems, or requires extensive cuts in walls, ceilings, or floors, you're better off bringing in a general contractor.

Be aware that once you hire a licensed electrician to perform work for you, he or she is required by law to identify and repair any existing electrical code violations that may exist. Unscrupulous electricians may confront you with several "violations" in areas totally unrelated to the work you contracted for. Insist on written estimates and descriptions for any such code-mandated work and ask for a photocopy of that part of the code that has allegedly been violated. Honest electricians will do work that's necessary, but won't go out of their way to search for violations. If you have any questions about whether the work is really necessary don't hesitate to call the local building department.

EXTERMINATORS

While almost every exterminator is licensed, that doesn't mean the individual actually doing the work in the home will be a skilled professional. Many licensed exterminators hire others to do the actual pesticide application. Insist the individual doing the application in your home be personally licensed and a member of the National Pest Control

Association. Similarly, ask for proof that the pesticides to be used are approved by the Environmental Protection Agency and find out what effect they'll have on woodwork, walls, and floors. Professionals will immediately ask whether you have young children or pets, and will explain whether or not you'll need to leave the premises. Most experienced exterminators base their fee on time and materials, so they will be hesitant to give anything other than a ballpark estimate over the telephone. The local humane society can be a good source for names of exterminators who specialize in large pests, such as raccoons or bats. Home inspectors should be able to recommend exterminators who specialize in eliminating insect infestations. Before signing any contract, check with references to make sure their problems were actually eliminated.

FENCING CONTRACTORS

Fencing specialists build chain link and wooden fences. (Masons build stone and brick walls.) The advantages of working with these contractors are that they can show you a wide variety of styles, sizes, and colors, and they're experienced at researching and working with lot lines and surveys. Fencing is sold by the running foot, but that price often does not include gates, top and bottom rails, or diagonal rails at corners. Insist on a full written description of exactly what is and isn't included in any price estimates. Bear in mind that local ordinances may stipulate how many gates are needed and where they must be located; the maximum height of fencing; and how close they can be to property lines. The most difficult part of any installation is the digging of postholes. The general rule of thumb is the higher the fence, the deeper the posts must go. They should penetrate below the local frost line, or at least thirty-six inches. Ask if there are any additional costs should they find rock when digging the postholes.

FIREPLACE AND WOOD STOVE INSTALLERS

In the past, fireplaces could only be installed by masons. But today there are zero-clearance fireplaces a carpenter can easily install in almost any home. These are so named because their special insulation allows them to be installed flush with existing woodwork and wallboards, rather than requiring a buffer of some form of masonry. A group of specialty contractors have sprung up to install wood stoves and these new fireplaces. Typically these are young carpenters who have been trained by a stove or fireplace manufacturer and who can also do a little roofing and a little drywalling. They work on referral from the stores, and often specialize in one or two particular brands.

The installation of a wood stove is usually very straightforward. Quoted prices, however, may not include tiling, which may be needed to bring the installation up to code. In fact, because stoves are so easy to install, building codes go into great detail about them. There are specifications for clearances from side and rear walls for both stoves and stovepipes. There are also mandated clearances for the chimney pipe, including distance from exterior and interior walls, and distance from the roof line.

Installing a zero-clearance fireplace is more complex and expensive than installing a wood stove, but it is still much simpler than retrofitting a masonry fireplace. The telltale sign of craftsmanship is how well the roofing work is done, so it's tough for a homeowner to make a judgment. You'll need to rely on references.

If you opt for a traditional masonry fireplace, be very

careful in selecting the mason. While any mason can build a chimney, one who builds a fireplace should have an added streak of artistry. Make sure you see examples of their previous work.

GARAGE BUILDERS

While any general contractor who could build an addition could also build a garage, there are a group of specialist contractors who do only this. Since they work on volume they allow almost no room for customizing. Each offers a series of plans in various styles and a menu of added features such as driveways, insulation, heating, nonskid flooring, different doors and windows, and electric openers. If one of their plans blends well with your home it makes sense to hire them. If their garages would stick out like a sore thumb, opt to commission plans from an architect and hire a traditional general contractor instead—there are few things worse than a garage out of character with its house. The best way to check craftsmanship is to examine prior jobs, paying particular attention to the detail work where high-speed contractors might cut a few corners. Be wary of any garage builder whose concrete slab floors exhibit cracking.

Garage builders often also build other outbuildings such as sheds and gazebos. Amenities such as working windows, doors, electricity, heat, insulation, and lighting generally cost extra. These outbuildings needn't be built on slabs—concrete block piers should be sufficient—but in all other respects they should be as solid as any other structure. Check if studs are spaced at sixteen inches on center; if pressure-treated lumber is used near the ground; and if there's sheathing under the exterior siding.

Gutter and Downspout Contractors

Gutter and downspout work is often done by siding or roofing contractors, though there are some specialists around. Typically referrals come from home centers or other contractors. Costs average four dollars a running foot for both gutters and downspouts, but can vary depending on the quality of aluminum or galvanized steel used. Insist on aluminum that's at least 1/40 of an inch thick, or 26-gauge steel. Real pros will examine the drainage around the house and suggest solutions to any problems, rather than simply replacing the existing system. They will also have their own portable gutter forming machine, which can form continuous length sections of gutters custom-fit to your home. This will help eliminate any leakage. If you've an old home with copper gutters and downspouts ask the local historical or preservation society for names of copper specialists. Copper gutters should always have soldered joints.

Heating, Ventilation, and Cooling Contractors

Because of the complex, multitrade nature of heating, ventilation, and cooling systems, contractors who specialize in them tend to be more like general contractors than subcontractors. A heating, ventilation, and cooling contractor is generally a plumbing contractor who also has a variety of specialists on call and who installs, services, and replaces gas, oil, and electrically-powered systems. Their crews can be large. For example: to work on forced-air heat systems they'll need sheet metal workers for the duct work; to work on steam systems they'll need steamfitters; and to work on hot-water systems they'll need hydronic engineers.

Most heating, ventilation, and cooling contractors are comfortable working directly with homeowners, and will submit written bids for major jobs. Repair work is generally charged by the hour. Since many work exclusively with one brand of product, this isn't a trade that allows for a lot of shopping around. But because there are very few visible signs of skill it would be tough to choose anyway. Look for someone who's a member of either the Mechanical Contractors Association of America, or the National Association of Plumbing, Heating, and Cooling Contractors. If you've an older home, make sure the contractor has experience retrofitting systems—it's much different than working with new construction. If you're going to incorporate some type of solar system in the home, look for a contractor who is also a member of the National Association of Solar Contractors.

HOUSEPAINTERS

When fresh, a cheap, single coat of watered down whitewash will look almost as good as a carefully applied three-coat job. Six months later, however, you'll be able to tell the difference. Simply put: A good painter is one who repairs problems before painting over them so the problems don't crop up again. For that reason, a professional painting job consists of a great deal of preparation—scraping flaking paint, patching cracks, sealing nail holes—before a coat of primer, and two coats of high-quality paint.

The best way to tell the difference between a summer moonlighter and a full-time professional is to see them at work. A professional will use heavy fabric drop cloths, long-handled brushes, and will work from large two-gallon buckets. When preparing the exterior of a house they'll cover all landscaping with drop cloths; use scaffolding if working in a crew; use power sprayers, scrub brushes, scrapers, and disk sanders to remove dirt, mildew, and old paint; and work only in the shade when the temperature is above 70 degrees.

If you can't see them on the job, look for these signs of quality work: even coats with no signs of brush marks or roller nap; no visible repairs; even lines where the gloss paint on trim meets the matte paint on walls or ceilings or where two different colors meet; and neatly painted window frames with paint in the joint where glass meets wood, but not on the pane itself.

Paint stores aren't good sources of names since they recommend only their customers. Instead, do a little nosing around, looking for homes with good paint jobs in the area, and ask who did the work. Historical societies are excellent sources for painters who do careful exterior work, and designers generally know good interior painters.

Insulation Contractors

It's fairly easy to insulate most modern homes since the products have even been designed for do-it-yourselfers. But retrofitting insulation in an older home is another matter. Decisions must be made on types of insulation to use, and how and where it should be installed. That's why specialists have sprung up. One good source of names is the local utility company. Look for someone who's a member of the Insulation Contractors of America.

The most common method of insulating an older home is to blow an insulating material (often composed primarily of ground-up newspaper) into the cavities between walls, floors, and ceilings. One sign of an experienced insulator is that they remove siding before drilling holes into the cavity, and then replace it so there are no visible signs of the job. Be very wary of spray-foam insulation. It is difficult to control the coverage of this material and if an area is missed it is nearly impossible to go back and respray. In addition, up until recently many of these foams contained the toxic material formaldehyde, so ask to see ingredient labels for any materials used.

LANDSCAPE CONTRACTORS

Not to be confused with landscape designers or landscape architects, these are the people who care for lawns, bushes, trees, and hedges. This is one of the easiest fields to enter—all you need is a lawn mower, a rake, a shovel, and a pickup truck—so the sign of a pro is experience. To survive in this business for a long time they must be providing quality service at a decent price. It's fairly easy to find a good landscaper since evidence of the quality of their work is all around us and entirely visible. Find a healthy, well-maintained, attractive garden and ask the homeowner who, if anyone, they have do their landscaping. (Don't worry if it turns out they do it themselves; you'll be paying them a terrific compliment by thinking otherwise.) It's a good sign if the landscaper is a member of the Associated Landscape Contractors of America, or the American Association of Nurserymen. Most landscapers charge a flat fee, based on size, for yard care and additional fees for plantings or special projects.

Some landscapers may also do other types of outdoor work such as tree surgery, fencing, or irrigation. If that's the case they should have additional credentials. For example: If they do tree surgery they should be a licensed arborist; and if they install sprinklers they should be a member of the Irrigation Association.

LOCKSMITHS

There's nothing wrong with turning to the Yellow Pages for the names of locksmiths. Look for someone who's a member of the Associated Locksmiths of America, and who's bonded, insured, and licensed. Make sure they use only UL-(Underwriter's Laboratory) listed products. And before hiring someone to do extensive work, ask the local police department for an opinion of past jobs.

MASONS

Masons do a lot more than just lay bricks. They build fireplaces, chimneys, stone and brick walls, foundations, and other concrete structures, as well as apply stone or brick veneers. While there are some masons, particularly in rural areas, who say they do all this work, most specialize in one or two areas. Therefore you should specialize in your hiring. If you're having a stone wall built around your property you don't want to hire a mason who does mostly fireplaces and chimneys. That's why the best source of names is from people who have had similar work done. If you're thinking of having a stone wall built, and pass by a particularly attractive one, stop in and ask for the name of the mason who did the work. And when you check their prior work, make sure it's the same type of job as you'll be having done.

When examining masonry work look for aesthetics first and craftsmanship second. Check if the mortar has been cleaned out to an equal depth and if there's discoloration from mortar spilling out of joints. Obviously, watch out for large cracks in foundations or slabs. Small cracks are to be expected in older work, but sizable gaps indicate poor preparation and/or workmanship. In metropolitan areas, membership in a union is a sign of professionalism. In suburban and rural areas look for a mason who's a member of the Mason Contractors Association of America.

PAPERHANGERS

Paperhanging is one of the few trades left that's predominantly self-taught. That's why the first major sign of professionalism is being in business for a long period of time. While many interior painters also hang wallpaper, top professionals specialize and rely almost exclusively on referrals from design professionals. The way the process generally works is, first you and your designer select a style of wallpaper. Then the paperhanger is called in to look at the room, see the type of paper being used, and give an estimate of how many rolls of paper will be needed. It's up to you to buy the materials. The paperhanger will also specify what condition the walls should be in when he or she arrives. They'll remove old wallpaper and prepare the walls if you wish, but they don't like to, and will make you pay handsomely for it. The best way to get an idea of a paperhanger's professionalism is to see them on the job. Pros will have their own portable paste-up tables, and will often use strap-on stilts to help them reach up to the ceiling. If you don't get a chance to see them on the job, look for how they handle switch and outlet plates. Skilled paperhangers will cover the plates with scrap paper, making sure the pattern matches the wall. While paperhangers can be a bit eccentric, their labor cost is small compared to the cost of paper, so it's worth hiring the best you can find.

PLASTERERS

A good plasterer can be very tough to find. Plastering has become a dying art ever since drywall construction took over, and those who still practice it charge handsomely. Experienced painters, general contractors who specialize in restorations, and local historical or preservation societies are probably the best sources for names. Because they're so tough to find and so expensive, other contractors may recommend you simply remove the old plaster and/or cover it with drywall rather than go through the time and effort of replastering. For minor plaster patch jobs it probably pays to have a painter do the work instead. But if you live in an old home and need to match some unusually ornate molding or cornice work, there's really no replacement for plaster. (If, on the other hand, you're just adding molding where none existed before, or are looking to replace plain molding, consider using mass produced plastic moldings. They look just fine once painted and cost much less.)

Plumbing Contractors

There's a big difference between plumbing contractors and plumbers. Plumbing contractors are insured, bonded, and licensed by the state and the local municipality. Plumbers, on the other hand, may have no licenses. Theoretically, plumbers can do work that doesn't affect public sewer or water lines, but my advice is to work only with plumbing contractors. As with electricians there are no visible signs of skill so you'll need to rely on references and accreditations. The plumbing contractor should be a member of the United Association of Plumbers and Pipe Fitters, and/or the National Association of Plumbing, Heating, and Cooling Contractors. Most plumbing contractors will provide written bids on all but the smallest project. They generally come up with their estimates by using a set price per fixture. Try to obtain your own fixtures, or at least settle on one particular common model, so you'll be better able to compare bids. Small repair jobs will be billed hourly. Many will ask for a deposit of up to 20 percent on smaller jobs. While you may not be able to negotiate the deposit away entirely you can probably talk them down to 10 or 15 percent instead. One word of warning: A plumbing contractor will only work on pipes. If the job involves wall, floor, or tile work as well, it's best to call in a general contractor.

PORCELAIN REFINISHERS

It makes sense to refinish, rather than replace, bathroom fixtures if they are: in good shape but their color doesn't match the new decor of the bathroom; functional but showing their age; or very difficult to replace. A good source for names is a local distributor of bathroom fixtures. Very often new fixtures are chipped in transit and the distributor needs to hire someone to repair them.

Porcelain refinishing is neither inexpensive nor simple. The surface must be etched, bonded, and then sprayed with a two-part primer and two-part top coat. Rather than actually using porcelain, which must be baked on, these specialists use either epoxy or polyurethane. In order to obtain the best results all trim and plumbing should be removed prior to etching. If a built-in fixture is being refinished, the grout line between it and the wall covering should be scraped out. The refinishing material needs to be extended into the gap and then regrouted to prevent water damage. Refinishing a tub costs approximately $300 and, because the various coats need time to cure, can take up to seventy-two hours. Even minor chips can take up to four hours to repair and cost around $150.

The sign of good workmanship is simple: If after a few

months you can't tell it was done, it was done well. A poorly done job will blister and peel rather quickly. Because few homeowners realize how complex and expensive this process actually is, and look on it instead as a quick fix, there are quite a few incompetents and shady operators passing themselves off as porcelain refinishers. Stick with established firms that have proven track records, since guarantees are only good for as long as a company remains in business. Be aware that even the best refinishing jobs are highly prone to chipping and scratching, especially if abrasive cleansers or steel wool are used.

RESILIENT-FLOOR LAYERS

Even though it requires some unique skills, the laying of vinyl or linoleum resilient flooring is often done by poorly paid, inexperienced laborers. Since installation is done by the seller of the floor, that makes it very important to work with a dealer who stands behind both their products and their services. Installation usually costs four dollars a square foot. A good dealer will investigate whether a subfloor is needed or an old floor must be removed. Uncaring dealers will simply install the new floor on top of the old. The signs of good workmanship are: a centrally located pattern; equal borders on all sides; no gaps between walls or cabinets and the flooring; even margins around obstructions like radiator pipes; flooring which extends under major appliances; and tight, flat, straight seams in unobtrusive areas.

ROOFING CONTRACTORS

Roofing has historically attracted more than its share of con artists for the simple reason that it's next to impossible for a homeowner to see what has been done to their roof. For this same reason it's necessary to see a roofing contractor on the job in order to make even a rudimentary judgment of their professionalism. Don't wait to find an old-timer. Roofing is a young person's profession requiring strength, agility, balance, and a good sunscreen. As they age, roofing contractors move into other carpentry-related trades. Signs of a pro are: wearing sneakers while working on granulated roofs; use of copper flashing sealed with solder around chimneys and vents; and use of a ladder with a mechanical lift to hoist shingles. Roofing installation is usually based on a "per square" price. A square is 100 square feet. This fee may or may not include the cost of shingles, but almost never includes the prep work.

Until a roofing contractor actually gets up on the roof, he or she can't tell how tough a job it will be. The existing decking under the shingles or the flashing may need to be replaced. In fact, proper preparation prior to shingle installation is a sure sign of an experienced hand. For example: If fiberglass or asphalt shingles are being used, a snow/ice shield should be installed first at the edges of the roof and where pitched roofs meet forming a valley. Then a prefabricated aluminum drip edge should be applied along the edges to protect them from weather damage. Next a layer of at least fifteen-pound roofing paper—also known as tar paper—should be added. Only after all this has been done should shingles be added.

If there's only one layer of shingles on the roof, a second can be added. But if there are already two layers they'll need to be removed since most local laws won't allow roofs to carry the weight of three layers. The type of shingle used will affect the price. Asphalt composition shingles and fiberglass shingles are the least expensive. Wood shingles and concrete tiles are moderately priced. Clay tiles and slate are the most expensive. (A word of warning: Not all roofing contractors have experience with all types of shingles.) There are even variations among types of shingles. The thicker and heavier a shingle the better it is and the longer it will last if properly installed. For example: asphalt shingles run from 200 to 300 pounds per square. Different shingles also have different degrees of fire resistance, Class A being the best.

If all this has you confused, I'm glad. I think it's a big mistake for a homeowner to hire a roofing contractor without a set of specifications prepared by an architect or home inspector.

SECURITY SYSTEM INSTALLERS

There's a tremendous range in the type of contractors who call themselves security dealers. Some make their living installing sophisticated, wired systems, while others install simple, wireless systems, and make their money by monitoring the system. That's why before calling any security contractors you must be very clear about what you want protected and how, and use that as a basis for bidding. If you opt for a wired system, look for a contractor who has experience working in the same type of home as yours. It's much easier to do wiring in new construction than in old plaster-walled homes. You don't want someone learning on your house. One sign of good workmanship is how well wiring is concealed. It can be difficult to compare bids since many dealers use different components, so rely heavily on the quality of references and the length of time the contractor has been in business. A good source for names is the local police department.

Many of these contractors have taken to calling themselves "low voltage specialists," and also install central vacuuming systems, telephone systems, intercoms, and home "brains" (computers which allow homeowners to control all of a home's systems from a remote location).

SIDING CONTRACTORS

These contractors install vinyl and aluminum siding. (Carpenters or specialists install wooden siding and cedar shakes.) When these products first hit the market they became notorious due to high-pressure salesmanship and shoddy installation. And although the industry has matured, there are still quite a few fly-by-night crews around. Siding contractors often rely on their very visible presence in a neighborhood to generate business. Installation cost is generally calculated by the square foot for the siding and by the linear foot for the eaves, soffits, and fascia boards. Preparation work is charged separately, usually by the hour. In order to come up with an accurate estimate the contractor must visit the site and examine the condition of the existing siding.

The best way to judge workmanship is to take a close look at previous jobs. Pay particular attention to the trim areas around doors and windows. They should be neat and tight. Look at the corners of the house. A good siding contractor will try to make sure the horizontal courses line up where walls meet. In a good job, siding joints will be placed in inconspicuous places, such as above doors and windows. Aluminum siding should be tight to the house, while vinyl siding should hang in place so there's room for it to expand and contract.

SUN SPACE AND GREENHOUSE BUILDERS

Home greenhouses, called sun spaces, are all the rage today, and in response, some general contractors are beginning to specialize in building them. In addition, many retailers and manufacturers of prefabricated sun spaces are training and sponsoring in-house and independent installers. Which type of contractor you use depends on whether or not you want to purchase a prefab unit or have one custom designed.

Price quotes generally don't include extras, such as heating, ventilation equipment, and shades, unless you specifically ask. When selecting a contractor to build a sun space ask for a list of clients from at least two years ago. Nearly all of these additions look good when brand-new. The key is how well they age and how responsive the contractor is to problems that crop up.

Since the construction is exposed it's fairly easy to check out the workmanship. All hardware and fasteners should be rust resistant. The wooden framing should be pressure-treated lumber. If possible glazing should be insulated, tempered, or laminated safety glass. Avoid acrylic plastics since they tend to scratch easily and discolor in the sun. If you must use plastic, insist on the use of Lexan —a high-end proprietary material manufactured by General Electric. Make sure whoever you deal with obtains all the necessary building permits. These structures, despite their shell-like appearance, are considered permanent by most building departments.

SWIMMING POOL AND POND BUILDERS

It can cost a small fortune to install an in-ground swimming pool or natural-looking pond, so it's essential the job be done right. These builders are actually specialized general contractors with excavators, masons, carpenters, plumbers, fencing contractors, landscapers, and electricians on staff. Since this is such a complex job, most contractors try to standardize it as much as possible by steering customers to particular brands, shapes, and styles. The trick, then, is to find someone who's willing to work with you in coming up with a design, rather than sell you something off the shelf. One sign of openness will be if they deal with a variety of suppliers and have done a wide range of jobs.

Look for a contractor who has done everything from vinyl-lined lap pools to free form, multidepth ponds. Aside from references, the best sign of professionalism is membership in the National Spa and Pool Institute. Plumbers and electricians on the contractor's staff should be fully licensed. A word of warning: Make sure price estimates include the entire package—excavation, moving of gas and electrical lines, installation, ladders, filters, diving boards, covers, lighting, decking, heating, and fencing. Also, be prepared for some surprise charges.

When I had my swimming pool built, I discovered there was a clause stipulating that blasting was extra. I didn't think anything of it until one afternoon when I received a call at my office from the contractor. He told me they had hit rock. I asked how much more it would cost to get rid of the rock. He explained the dynamiting would cost a minimum of eight thousand dollars. I thought of how my backyard would look with a huge pile of earth and an exposed pit, gritted my teeth, and told him to blast away.

TELEVISION ANTENNA AND SATELLITE SYSTEM CONTRACTORS

The installation of TV antennas is generally included as part of the purchase of the unit, since it almost always makes more sense to replace rather than repair an antenna. It usually costs around two hundred dollars to have a roof antenna installed and hooked up to a single television. Multiple hookups and rotating systems obviously cost more, and interior wiring is more expensive than exterior wiring.

When having a satellite system installed check first with local municipalities for the rules and regulations. Then compare that information to what salespeople tell you to get a reading on a company's honesty. While your reception has less to do with the installation than the quality of the equipment, there are some things to watch out for. Be wary of companies that promise reception of certain channels and quote you installation costs without first visiting the site. Insist any trimming of landscaping be done only on your okay and that the channels and stations you'll receive be stipulated in the contract. Ask references whether or not they receive all the channels promised in the sales pitch and the contract.

TILE LAYERS

While many other contractors may claim to be able to do tile work, it's actually a very specialized skill. Experienced full-time tile layers generally base their price estimates on the square footage of the area to be covered. The signs of good workmanship are: symmetrical layouts in which the outside tiles are all approximately the same size; even spacing between tiles; a level surface; and uncracked and sealed grout that's between, not on the surface of, the tiles. It's usually a big mistake for a homeowner to hire a tile layer directly since the long-term success of the job depends as much on the underlayment and preparation of the floor prior to tiling (work that is generally done by a carpenter) as it does on the tiling itself. For example: Wall and ceiling tiles in showers and tub areas should be installed only on a highly moisture resistant, cement-type wallboard called "wonder board." Other tiling in bath-rooms and kitchens should be done on a moisture resistant Sheetrock called "green board." The only time tiles should be installed on standard Sheetrock is if they are purely decorative and will not come in contact with moisture. It take more than two days for a tile job to cure, so schedul-ing becomes very important. As with paperhanging, the labor cost of tiling is low compared to the material cost, so it makes sense to hire only the best.

WELL-DRILLING CONTRACTOR

It's actually quite easy to select a good well-drilling con-tractor. Simply ask them how long they've been in busi-ness. No one stays in the well-drilling business for very long if they don't find water. Make sure they're a Certified Well-Driller or a Certified Pump Installer, as well as a member of the National Well Water Association. If you're also having them install water filtration or treatment equipment, check to see that they are also a member of the Water Quality Association. Make sure to include a clause in your contract with them stipulating that they will stop drilling as soon as they hit sufficient water. Otherwise, some well drillers will continue to drill to the contracted depth even if they hit water much shallower.

WINDOW REPLACEMENT SPECIALISTS

Like many of the other specialized carpentry trades, these contractors work on volume. While not completely inat-tentive to detail, the secret to their success is that they can come in and completely replace a home's windows in a very short time. Some also repair older windows. The se-cret to your satisfaction will actually depend on how much accuracy they sacrifice in their quest for speed. Most depend on home center referrals for the bulk of their business. Cost will depend on how much detail work is involved in the job. For example: The per window charge will increase if they're going to reuse original trim. Ask prior customers if they've experienced any draft or leakage problems, and check how well the trim and moldings match up. Don't become too obsessive, however. Your happiness with the job will probably depend more on the quality of windows you've bought than on the quality of their craftsmanship.

WINDOW WASHERS

The professionalism of window washers depends on location. In urban areas where there are a great many high-rise buildings, there will be a good number of professional firms who specialize in washing windows. In suburban areas there will probably be a handful of firms that deal regularly with shopkeepers. But in rural areas you'll probably need to rely on a part-timer who has no fear of heights. Costs vary by region, but are almost always calculated as a flat fee per window. Make sure the charge includes cleaning both the inside and outside of the windows. If some windows must be cleaned from the outside, and you've hired a part-timer, make certain your homeowner's insurance provides adequate coverage, because you can rest assured they won't have coverage.

WOOD-FLOOR SANDERS, REFINISHERS, AND INSTALLERS

This is the specialized trade with probably the greatest disparity between craftsmen. On the one hand there are individuals who lease a sanding machine and declare themselves professionals, while on the other hand there are highly skilled finish carpenters who do exquisite work. While a general contractor will be able to easily tell the difference, it's much tougher for an inexperienced homeowner. Professional refinishing jobs involve: sinking exposed nails; multiple passes with various size machines and grades of sandpaper followed by vacuuming; two coats of oil; and finally two coats of polyurethane. The job can be very messy, so most experienced craftsmen use plastic to seal off the room from the rest of the house. Pros will generally avoid giving price estimates until they see the room in question.

The same individuals who refinish existing wood floors often install new ones. An experienced wood-floor installer will use a special tool that allows them to avoid nailing through the face of boards—a technique known as "blind nailing." Even those few nails that do need to be hammered through the face of boards will be made invisible through countersinking and filling with wood putty. After most truly professional jobs you won't be able to see a single nail head.

The exception is when a rustic look is desired. When laying rustic-style soft wood floors with either wide-plank or random-width pine, some combination of blind and face nailing is the preferred method. The face nailing will often be done with decorative forged nails. The standard-cut nails will be countersunk, but the heads of the decorative nails will remain partially exposed. If you're contemplating a rustic floor, insist on getting a mock-up (at least 6 feet × 6 feet) so you get some idea of the arrangement of boards and their spacing. While some space between boards is in keeping with the rustic style, there shouldn't be any gaps larger than ⅛-inch since the wood will eventually shrink.

WROUGHT-IRON CONTRACTORS

Wrought-iron work is strictly customized, and referrals are almost entirely by word of mouth. When you contact a firm they will send a salesman with a sample book to your home. He or she will take some measurements and make suggestions on appropriate styles, showing you photos of similar jobs. Don't be shy about asking for prices. Elaborate wrought-iron work can be very costly, so it's best to give the salesperson an idea of your price range early on. Try to select a common design in order to be able to compare prices.

SUBCONTRACTOR FEES

Here's a chart that will give you an idea of what some individual subcontractors charge by the hour, how they come up with their prices, and how much room you have to negotiate. The information is based on data supplied by R.S. Means. The first column contains an average of the base union labor hourly rates for individual trades in thirty major U.S. cities. The second column is their total average overhead. These numbers are for contractors with billings of $500,000—in other words, a moderate-size operation. Actual overhead will vary depending on the exact size of the contractor, support costs and staff requirements, job logistics, and economic conditions. The third column contains a 10 percent profit figure. The fourth column is the total of the previous three, representing the hourly rate a consumer would pay. It's safe to assume that contractors eager for work will be willing to reduce their profit margin somewhat, so you may be able to cut into the 10 percent figures in the third column. Be wary of contractors willing to reduce fees so much that they cut into their overhead, however: They may go out of business, or quit, in the middle of your project.

Trade	Base Rate	Overhead	Profit	Hourly Fee
Asbestos worker	25.50	12.10	2.55	$40.15
Bricklayer	23.40	10.00	2.35	$35.75
Bricklayer's helper	18.15	7.75	1.80	$27.70
Carpenter	22.85	10.40	2.30	$35.55
Common laborer	18.00	8.20	1.80	$28.00
Demolition crew member	18.00	11.70	1.80	$31.50
Electrician	26.10	10.25	2.60	$38.95
Floor tile layer	22.70	8.30	2.30	$33.30
Floor tile layer's helper	18.20	6.70	1.80	$26.70
Glazier	23.05	9.30	2.30	$34.65
Lather	22.75	8.80	2.30	$33.85
Light-equipment operator	22.30	9.25	2.25	$33.80
Marble setter	23.20	9.95	2.30	$35.45
Millwright	23.60	9.05	2.40	$35.05
Mosaic and terrazzo worker	22.90	8.40	2.30	$33.60
Painter	21.30	8.70	2.10	$32.10
Paperhanger	21.50	8.80	2.10	$32.40
Plasterer	22.35	9.40	2.25	$34.00
Plasterer's helper	18.40	7.75	1.85	$28.00
Plumber	26.45	10.80	2.65	$39.90
Roofer—composition	20.85	11.95	2.10	$34.90
Roofer's helper	15.10	8.70	1.50	$25.30
Roofer—tile and slate	20.95	12.05	2.10	$35.10
Sheet-metal worker	25.75	11.35	2.60	$39.70
Stone mason	23.60	10.10	2.35	$36.05

CHAPTER 8

Analyzing Bids and Making a Decision

———

It's not what you pay a man but what
he costs you that counts.
—WILL ROGERS

The bids you receive from general contractors reflect more than just the estimated cost of the project. They're windows into the general contractors' businesses and minds. As I explained earlier in my description of the bids from the three different-size general contractors, motivation and knowledge of all the project entails are also reflected in the bottom line. In addition, the ability, motivation, and knowledge of the subcontractors can be discerned. The bids also follow the economic health of the community. Before you actually examine and compare the individual bids, let me explain how they're actually put together.

The general contractor will initially make a rough estimate of what she believes the job will cost, based on her experience. She'll then decide which individual trades will be required. Next, she'll call in her favorite subcontractors, provide them with a copy of the plans and specifications, and ask them to come up with a price based on the plans. The individual subcontractors will price out their part of the job, including the fixtures and materials they'll need. Most will come up with labor prices based on simple rules of thumb they learned from older craftsmen: plumbers will charge a certain amount per fixture, and electricians a set price per outlet, switch, or fixture, for example. Their set prices may fluctuate a bit, however, depending on how much work they've already lined up. When they're busy, for example, plumbers may bid at $50 per fixture. But if things are slow they may drop their price to $45 or even $40. The general contractor will add in the costs of laborers she may need to hire to do the noncrafts work—delivery, unloading, cleaning up—and come up with a subtotal. Then she'll add in her overhead and profit and come up with a total.

But that may not be the number you see on the bottom line. When a general contractor bids on your job, she'll know she's not alone. After taking a look at your comprehensive plans and specifications, providing the information you've asked for, and being told you want a fixed, or budget, price, the general contractor will realize you're no pushover, and will undoubtedly be getting other bids. And if all that wasn't enough, the two other file folders sitting on your kitchen table will make it quite clear. By turning the bidding process into a competition, you force the general contractor to decide how much she wants the job. If she's eager for the job she may go back to her subcontractors and encourage them to reduce their fees. Then she'll start working on her own. The more she wants or needs the job, the more she and her subcontractors will be willing to cut their profit margins.

Bearing all this in mind, let's compare the individual bids. You wouldn't be human if you didn't first look at the bottom lines. Don't worry about them individually. Look at them as a group instead.

Are they all well above the budget you presented to your designer? If you've followed all the rules about selecting the right size general contractors, and the lowest bid is more than 15 percent above the figure you gave the professional who drew up your plans, the problem must be with your plans. Telephone all the general contractors, tell them what has happened, apologize, and promise to get back to them with amended plans within a week. Then get on the telephone with your planning professional and let them have it. Express your annoyance and concern and say you need another set of plans closer to the cost level you had requested. Point out any cost-cutting suggestions the candidate general contractors made in their bids. Stress you need it as soon as possible. If only minor changes are required there will probably be no charge. When you receive the revamped plans call back your general contractor candidates and ask for new bids. If major changes must be made, avoid the temptation to switch planning professionals. Even though you'll probably be forced into paying additional design fees, if you switch professionals now you could set the project back two months or more. If you're forced into cutting back on your project, opt to narrow its scope rather than to degrade the quality: scale down rather than go second class. It's better to do two rooms the way they should be done, rather than do four rooms in a half-baked manner. You can always get back to those other two rooms sometime in the future.

If it looks like the general contractors were bidding on three different jobs, it could once again be a problem with your plans. On the other hand, it could mean you've fallen into the Goldilocks trap and haven't picked the right size general contractors. Double-check with your planning professional that the general contractors are all of a similar size. If they are, the problem is your plans are leaving too much up to the general contractors. Telephone all the bidders, explain the situation, and tell them you'll have another set of more specific plans for them to rebid on shortly. Then tell your planning professional to make the original plans more specific.

If only one bid is dramatically higher or lower than the other two, don't worry. While it indicates desperation, lack of interest, or a complete misreading of the plans by that general contractor—none of which are good—it reflects on him, not you or your designer. And after all, that's the purpose of the bidding process.

Leave the bottom lines for now and take a look at the individual prices for subcontractors. First, make sure all three bids list the same kinds of subcontractors. If one general contractor failed to account for a necessary trade, or if the reverse occurs, and only one general contractor sees the need to bring in a particular trade, flag that line of the bid. Either the general contractor has made a mistake, has spotted something the others didn't, or has added an unnecessary expense to your bill. The only way to find out will be to ask him about it later. Don't be surprised if some of the subcontractor bids are identical. The general contractors may have actually gone to the same subcontractor. In any case, they should all be fairly close. If there are any subcontractor prices that seem out of line with the rest, either substantially higher or lower, flag them for later discussion. The general contractor can always go back and get a more accurate or more reasonable bid from another subcontractor.

Now turn to the general contractor's fee. If all your general contractors do the same size jobs, and run the same size operation, their overheads should be very close. One may drive a Chevy pickup, and another a Jeep Cherokee, but as long as none of them tools around in a Jaguar, you can assume the differences in their fee reflect different profit margins. And since they're all operating in the same economic environment, their need for work in general should be similar. That means any differences in contractor fees reflect their eagerness to do the job. And if all other things are equal, the person who's most eager will usually work the hardest.

Telephone all the general contractors, and ask them about any items you've flagged. Either get a plausible explanation for each discrepancy, or ask them for another price. Don't try to negotiate their own fee or profit downward. Squeezing the general contractor means squeezing the job. A disgruntled general contractor and crew won't do quality work, and will jump ship at the first opportunity.

Contact your planning professional (or whoever will be supervising the job) and ask them to take a look at the bids. First, ask them to double-check that each general contractor has followed the specifications. Then, ask them to take a very good look at your lowest bidder. Tell them everything you know about their financial solvency and credit worthiness, and explain what you saw and found out from visiting past jobs. Before you can even consider the low bid, you need to know the general contractor hasn't underbid so far they've put themselves and the success of the project in jeopardy. Next, ask them to study the highest bid. Has this general contractor, or one of his subcontractors, discovered something about the project the other two missed? Has he been realistic while the others have been optimistic? Or is he just not as motivated?

Now comes the hard part: reaching a decision. There are lots of so-called rules about choosing a bidder. Perhaps the most popular is the "throw out the top and the bottom and choose the middle" rule. However, there's also the "you get what you pay for" rule that advises selecting the highest bidder—as long as he's not too high. Finally, there's the old reliable "don't look a gift horse in the mouth" rule that advocates grabbing the low bid.

I don't believe any of these rules make much sense. Each bidding process, every design, and all general contractors are different. There's no hard and fast rule about which to choose. Instead, you need to balance and weigh four factors: experience, motivation, skill, and cost. Try not to let personality play too much of a role in your decision. While it's nice to like your general contractor, it's more important to feel he or she's the one most likely to do the job well, and to come as close as possible to the schedule and budget.

Sometimes it's easy to forget craftsmanship isn't everything. I remember one client of mine who fell in love with the artistry of a struggling young general contractor. The young man had a winning personality. He came to my client and explained he'd be able to provide a better bid if my client purchased their own materials. A blinking red light signaling financial insolvency went off in my head, but my client would hear nothing of it. My client went to the wholesaler and paid cash for the materials. The general contractor, who did fine work, still couldn't keep his head above water. He kept getting deeper and deeper in the hole, until finally he told my client he couldn't continue the job—he'd run out of money and credit. It was all I could do to restrain my client from injecting capital into the young man's business.

A general contractor going broke in the middle of a job isn't uncommon. According to the National Association of Home Builders, 80 to 90 percent of all contractors are out of business within five years. If your general contractor goes broke it may cost you twice the original price to get someone else in to finish the job. That's why I advise you to avoid trying to prop up a general contractor financially. Even if he's the Leonardo of carpenters, you shouldn't hire him as your general contractor if he's not a good businessman.

Since this is such a customized process I don't feel comfortable telling you which of the bidders you should pick. However, I can tell you how I've made my choices. As long as the lowest bidder is competent, financially solvent, and seems to understand the job, that's who I select.

It's natural if after making your selection you still have a few qualms. Don't lose too much sleep over it. You're going to be protected by an airtight contract.

SAMPLE GENERAL CONTRACTOR BID

The following is an actual example of a general contractor's bid on a major renovation project. I've selected such a substantial job in order to show you the range of individual elements that could be contained in a bid. The only things I have changed are the names of the residence and the contractor.

PROJECT: SMITH RESIDENCE
CONTRACTOR: JONES ENTERPRISES INC.

Base Bid:

1.	General conditions	$17,310
2.	Site work, excavation, demolition	23,185
3.	Concrete work	3,055
4.	Masonry	5,540
5.	Framing	38,270
6.	Insulation	4,400
7.	Stucco	15,690
8.	Roofing, gutters, etc.	35,820
9.	Doors and hardware	12,080
10.	Windows	14,975
11.	Drywall, taping, etc.	8,160
12.	Finish carpentry, wood flooring	13,025
13.	Ceramic tile	9,315
14.	Plumbing	17,595
15.	Heating	15,520
16.	Electrical	10,160
17.	Other (toilet accessories, medicine cabinets)	675
	Total	$244,785

We will start work within two weeks or earlier after execution of the contract if the building permit is issued. It will take eighteen weeks to complete the project as per the drawings and specifications.

Alternate #1—Kitchen Cabinet Installation
Install kitchen cabinets as shown (provided by owner)
Add $2,645 and 2 days

Alternate #2—Garage
Strip interior wall and ceiling plaster in garage and install new gypsum board walls and ceiling. Gypsum board to be two layers of ⅝" fire code gypsum board.
Add $1,700 and 5 days

Alternate #3—Stair
Modify existing stair as per detail No. 5, Sheet A-15
Deduct $1,700 and 2 days

Alternate #4—Air Conditioning
Provide central air conditioning unit with air handler over bath #2 and ducted supply and return to all second floor rooms except hall and stair. Condenser to be located at corner of garage and kitchen.
Add $7,560 and 5 days

Alternate #5—Electrical Service
Provide new 200-amp electrical service with new circuit breaker panel.
Add $1,725 and 2 days

Alternate #6—Interior Doors and Trim
All interior doors, frames, door trim, baseboards, and miscellaneous wood trim to be clear pine. Railings to be oak.
Deduct $5,195

As you can see the general contractor has provided a breakdown of each element that goes into the total project. This would allow for a line by line comparison with other bids for both amounts and for which trades were involved. If, for example, the electrical line of this bid were much higher than the electrical line of others, the general contractor could be asked to have the electrical work rebid. The line for general conditions is the visible portion of the general contractor's fee. Other portions of his profit and overhead are probably built into the lines for portions of the job that his own staff may be handling, such as framing and finish carpentry.

Note that the general contractor has also included alternatives to the plans that could either improve or cut the cost of the job. For example, to add central air conditioning to the project (alternate #4) would increase the price by $7,560 and the time required by five days. On the other hand, if interior doors and trim (alternate #6) were made of clear pine rather than the oak that was probably indicated in the plans, the cost of the project could be reduced by $5,195. This alternate, which the general contractor has probably listed last in order to close his bid with a bang, shows real insight.

The architect in this project probably specified oak doors and trim throughout the addition since the rest of the woodwork in the home was oak. The general contractor, realizing that much of this trim would be painted over, rightly concludes that it is crazy to pay for oak and then paint it, when clear pine would give the same effect. The only trim the general contractor suggests keeping as oak are the railings. That's probably because they are going to be stained rather than painted. Showing the homeowner how they could save over $5,000 with no visible effect on the job probably won this project for the general contractor.

CHAPTER 9

Drafting the Contract

___

*It is a bad plan that admits no
modification.*
—PUBLILIUS SYRUS

Some general contractors
use their bidding form as a
contract to perform the job as well as to provide an estimate. But these are at best vague and at worst meaningless
agreements, offering little or no protection for the consumer. Many general contractors go one step further and
use a standard form contract drawn up by the American
Institute of Architects. While these are more equitable than
the traditional bid/contracts, they are still not sufficient.

My advice is to have your own attorney draft a simple
agreement spelling out, in detail, the rights and responsibilities of both parties. (For a sample of such a contract see

pages 213 through 228.) It will take an experienced attorney no more than four hours to prepare such an agreement—less if he has one already on file. Since legal fees range widely from $75 to $250 per hour, such a project will cost anywhere from $300 to $1,000. I honestly believe it's money well spent. However, if your job is too small to justify the expense, you can ask your attorney to amend the general contractor's AIA form. That should take no more than an hour and cost you from $75 to $250. (For a description of the changes your attorney is likely to make see page 183.) Despite the added cost, having a professionally drafted, or altered, contract is essential. Without it, you're just asking for trouble. Remember that you're, in effect, surrendering control of your home—your most precious asset—to another party. You'd never rent your home without having a lease, so why hand it over to a construction crew without an equitable contract?

The contract should include a discussion of all the financial terms, including the total price, the down payment, when further payments are to be made, and how large they'll be. The main point for contention here will be the size of the down payment. Obviously, general contractors will want as much up front as possible. However, it should be possible to limit the down payment to not more than 10 percent of the total price.

To the fullest extent possible throughout the contract and during the actual job, you want to remain ahead of the general contractor. In other words, you want him to have done more work and/or supplied more materials than he's actually been paid for. One of the worst things a homeowner can do is let a general contractor get ahead of them. If a general contractor has been paid for 25 percent of a job, but has only done 15 percent of the actual work, there's nothing stopping him from pulling the crew off the job for a couple of days to work somewhere else. Even if you cancel the project, he and his subcontractors are ahead of the game.

The best way to avoid this all too common nightmare is to contractually tie payments to particular stages of the job. For example: the contract should state when 25 percent of the work has been completed, X dollars will be paid; when 50 percent has been done, Y dollars will be paid; and when 75 percent is finished, Z dollars will be paid. And the decision as to when those stages have been reached should be made by the professional who's supervising the job, not the general contractor. Another clause should stipulate that no monies will be paid out until a representative of the municipality, or the owner's supervisory professional, inspects the work and certifies that it has been done in accordance with local codes and regulations.

To further insure you remain ahead of the general contractor, your contract should stipulate you'll be keeping a 10 percent retainage. That means you'll withhold 10 percent of each scheduled payment, including the final payment, until 30 days after your supervisory professional certifies the project is finished. This way you'll have some leverage to get the general contractor to come back to correct problems.

You can try to sneak through a clause stipulating the general contractor will devote full-time to your project, and/or that the job be "continuously prosecuted," but don't be surprised if she objects. Insist, however, on a provision declaring that the general contractor cannot assign the contract to someone else. At least then you're sure the person you've chosen will also be the person who does the job.

The contract should also have a clause requiring the general contractor to obtain and maintain adequate insurance coverage. As evidence, the general contractor should be required to provide an insurance certificate from his insurer. This is a form an insurance company issues, indicating that it has been informed about the project and acknowledges its coverage.

The contract should include at least two supplements, the first containing a complete description of the project—including all the work to be performed and a list of all the materials to be used. The description of the materials should include brand and model names, size, color, quantities, and any other descriptive features. The second supplement should be a listing of the charges for extras added to the plan prior to beginning work and for changes made to the plan once the project is underway. Both these supplements will probably take the form of your finalized plans and specifications and the general contractor's finalized and accepted bid package.

Make sure the agreement also contains a clause specifying that you must approve any changes to the materials list if an item becomes unavailable, as well as a provision allowing you to buy materials on your own, and requiring the general contractor to pass along any savings.

Another provision in the agreement should state that you or your supervisory professional will be provided with proof that the subcontractors and material suppliers are actually being paid by the general contractor. In many states, if a subcontractor or supplier isn't paid by a general contractor, he or she can attach a mechanics lien on the home and require the homeowner to pay the bill, even if the general contractor has already been paid.

One section of the agreement should discuss start and finish dates. Since you're asking for a budget price, it's probably unreasonable to also ask for a fixed completion date. Instead, an approximate date should be stated, along with bonuses and penalties for early or late completion.

Remember: General contractors' estimates of how long a job will take are best case scenarios predicted on no surprises. Also, good general contractors and subcontractors are in demand and have busy schedules—they may not be able to fit you in exactly when you'd like. If for some reason your project must be completed by a specific date, you'll probably need to eliminate your demand for a fixed fee and instead let the general contractor work on time and materials, but with a guarantee of completion by a certain time.

There should be language in the contract that stipulates that all work will be performed in a "good and workmanlike" manner, in accordance with all applicable building codes, and that the general contractor will obtain all necessary permits. If you wish the general contractor to be responsible for cleaning up, removing debris, and protecting materials, it should be stated in the agreement.

Another clause in the contract should state that any irreconcilable disputes between you and the general contractor must be resolved either through the auspices of the National Association of Home Builders or by the American Arbitration Association. I'll fully explain the reasons for this clause in chapter 11, but for now let's just say that the only people who actually win in litigation are the lawyers.

Finally, an entire portion of the contract should be devoted to the terms and conditions of warranties on both materials and workmanship. It should state the warranties the general contractor will herself provide on her subcontractors' work, and that all manufacturers' warranties will be turned over to you. The names and addresses of the individuals or companies who will honor these warranties should be listed in a third supplement.

Make sure there is a clause making the general contractor personally responsible for the job. Many general contractors have their own private corporations, which are nothing more than paper shields against personal liability. Some general contractors create and dissolve corporations each season. To insure that you have some recourse, the general contractor should provide a personal as well as corporate guarantee.

Once you and the general contractor sign the contract, you can take a couple of days off to relax. But don't become complacent. You now must figure out where you're going to get the money to pay the general contractor.

CUSTOM HOME RENOVATION CONTRACT

The appendix on pages 213–228 gives an example of a custom contract that includes all of the provisions and clauses discussed in this chapter. In addition, a short letter contract reinforcing the fact that your planning professional will provide job supervision is also included on pages 229–230. This letter serves to link all your contracts and professionals together, and is advisable. Because the circumstances surrounding each home-renovation project are different, the contract and letter are included as samples and may require modifications to address the specific details of your renovation.

AMENDING THE AIA FORM CONTRACT

While it is surprisingly evenhanded for a form contract, the AIA contract between an owner and a contractor has three critical areas that need to be expanded on: job commencement and substantial completion dates (and their penalties and premiums); payment schedules; and periodic inspections.

TIMING, PENALTIES, AND PREMIUMS

The AIA form is very skimpy when it comes to stating exactly when jobs will be started and finished. Therefore, firm commencement and substantial completion dates should be inserted. In addition, a clause imposing penalties of a specified amount for each day beyond the completion date should be added. In order to get the general contractor to agree to this, a clause providing for a specified premium for early completion may need to be added as well.

Most general contractors will also want to add what is called a "force majeure" clause. This gives them additional time to complete a project if unforeseen emergencies—such as hurricanes, strikes, or labor shortages—occur. Insist this clause be carefully worded to allow extra time for true "acts of God," like hurricanes, but not for delays caused by the general contractor him- or herself.

PAYMENT SCHEDULE

The AIA form says almost nothing about payment schedules. It should be amended so that, aside from an initial good faith down payment, the owner doesn't pay the general contractor until various stages in the project are completed. Some exceptions can be made. For example, if the general contractor must make a sizable payment for materials to be delivered to the job site. But other than possible payment for supplies, progress payments should be structured so they equal the value of the work completed, less 10 percent held back as retainage until the entire job is done.

PERIODIC INSPECTIONS

The AIA form requires the general contractor to complete
the work in a good and workmanlike manner in accordance with all local ordinances and codes, but does not
contain a provision stipulating interim inspections, either
by the building department or a third party job supervisor.
A clause should be added that before any payments are
made, all work up until that point must be inspected by a
representative of the local municipality or the owner, and
certified as being done in accordance with all local codes
and requirements.

CHAPTER 10

Obtaining Financing

———

*A financier is a pawnbroker with
imagination.*

—ARTHUR WING PINERO

Even though you know you can afford to pay for this renovation, based on your analysis early on, that doesn't mean the financial work is over. You still need to get the money. And while there is still plenty of money out there in the marketplace, lenders are being especially careful today.

Regardless of what type or size loan you'll be applying for, the lender will be checking your credit file. That's why you should beat them to the punch and check it for any potential problems. (For information on how to obtain copies of your credit files see page 192.) If you find mistakes or omissions, contact the credit bureau or the creditor and have them cleared up as soon as possible. If there are any negative judgments of your past performance, try to explain them in a one-hundred-word statement that will then be added to your file. With your credit report spruced up, or at least on the way, you can begin shopping for a loan.

Whichever type of financing technique you choose, it's essential to compare loans. Mortgages, home-equity, and home improvement loans are three of the most profitable and safe types of loans a bank can make. For that reason, there's a great deal of competition for the business. In order to set themselves apart, banks create their own unique products and establish their own lending rules. Of course, they present these in the best possible light. In order to be certain you're getting the best deal you must spend some time studying the various alternatives.

Shopping for Loans

Initially, installment loans may appear to be straightforward. The bank gives you a specific amount of dollars and you promise to pay a certain amount back each month for a predetermined period of time. However, there can be many variations. For example: the way banks calculate and express interest, and compute finance charges. Let's say you borrow $10,000. Your finance charge is $500, so you'll end up with $9,500 in your pocket. Bank A may charge interest on only the $9,500 you receive, while Bank B may charge interest on the entire $10,000. Banks may have different lending policies. Even branches of the same bank may have different policies depending on their clientele. A downtown branch of Bank A, which has many struggling artists, writers, dancers, and musicians among its depositors, may readily make loans to self-employed individuals, while an uptown branch of the same bank, which has mostly wealthy depositors, may not.

Call several banks in your area. Don't just stick to the big names—contact local, regional, foreign, and ethnic banks as well. Explain that you're interested in obtaining information on either a home improvement or a personal loan (depending on whether you've any equity in your home), and state the amount you need. Ask for the average percentage rate (APR) on each loan product. This is the actual interest rate you'll be paying, unobscured by fine print or marketing hype, and banks are required by law to provide it to you. If the loan has a variable interest rate, find out which index it's tied to, and do some research on its past behavior. Get information on how finance charges are computed, and on the bank's requirements for approval. Ascertain how much your monthly payment would be. In the final analysis, base your decision on which loan to apply for on the amount of the monthly payment, with the APR a close second.

Some general contractors, particularly specialty general contractors such as garage builders, offer installment loan financing as part of their package. I'd steer clear of such contractor-financed arrangements. You should select a general contractor based on their skill, solvency, and track record, not on the APR of their proposed loan. Just as it's important to keep the design and construction functions apart, so should financing be an entirely separate matter.

Shopping for first and second mortgages is a bit more complicated than looking for installment loans. Compile a comprehensive list of the lending institutions in your area that offer them. That could take you a while, since not only will the list include savings banks and still solvent savings and loans, but also commercial banks, finance companies, and credit unions. Check the Yellow Pages for the names of any local mortgage compilation services who could do this preliminary legwork for you. Telephone each potential lender and ask to speak to a loan officer. Be friendly: You've a great many questions to ask and will be on the telephone with this individual for quite some time. Every potential lender probably has two or three different products to fit your needs, so make sure you get information on each offering. Make one copy of the worksheet at the end of this chapter for each potential lender, and use them to keep track of all the data. After you've compiled all the information, compare the options and, with the help of your financial advisor, decide which best suits your needs.

After you've picked a target bank, stop by, ask for the same person you spoke to on the telephone, say hello, and ask for an application. Whether applying for a home-equity loan, a new first mortgage, a home improvement loan, or a personal loan, it's helpful to have a contact at the bank—someone who can shepherd your application through the red tape.

FILLING OUT LOAN APPLICATIONS

Loan applications are all fairly similar. They're long, complex documents designed to determine your willingness and ability to pay back a loan. The questionnaires typically ask for a list—and proof—of your assets, including bank accounts; your gross salary; other sources of income; obligations and outstanding debts. There will also be questions on how long you've lived in your current home, and how long you've held your current job. The reason these questionnaires are so in-depth is that they're designed to take the place of a personal interview. And the reason they seem to dwell on lengths of time is that banks equate personal and financial stability.

In the old days, bankers used to sit down with potential borrowers, talk with them, take a reading on their personality and character, and make a decision based on their impressions. Today, for better or worse, banks no longer conduct such interviews. Instead, they use a system called scoring to determine whether or not you qualify for a loan. Every answer on your application is assigned a numerical value. In order to qualify for a loan your application answers must total out to a certain score. Clerks are told the numerical equivalents for answers and are instructed to simply come up with a total score.

In an effort to make it easier to calculate your score, and to allow a clerk to figure it out, the application generally asks yes/no questions, or for lengths of time, and provides a very limited amount of space for responses. You can maximize your chances of acceptance, even in times when lenders are being extra cautious, by throwing a monkey wrench into this scoring process. The first time you reach a question the answer to which you feel requires some explanation, write "See Supplement A," rather than a response. On a separate sheet of paper, type your full answer, under the title Supplement A. As you move through the application, do the same with other answers that should be expanded, adding more and more supplements to your application.

When your application is received, a clerk will see it's out of the ordinary and won't know what to do with it. They're only trained and allowed to make objective decisions. They'll hand your application to their supervisor, someone who can make subjective decisions. The supervisor will then be able to read your supplements, and assign a score based on a subjective, rather than objective, analysis.

Let me give you an example of how this works. Since scoring systems generally equate job stability with personal stability, they assign higher scores to individuals who have been at the same job for a long period of time. If you've changed jobs two times in the past five years you'll automatically receive a lower score. But what if such job-hopping is common in your industry, and with each shift came a substantial increase in salary? Bringing such information to the attention of a decision-maker could turn a potential negative into a positive, and perhaps spell the difference between acceptance and rejection.

As soon as you finish preparing your customized application, bring it to the bank. Rather than simply dropping it on a desk, ask to meet with your "shepherd." Explain to them your application is special, and point out your supplements. If you've made efforts to clean up your credit file, show proof of them. Plaintively ask them to keep an eye on your application as it moves through the bank's bureaucracy. Also ask if it would be all right for you to call them if you've any questions. By now, your shepherd will have attached a name and face to the application package, insuring you get fair treatment.

Hopefully, all the care and attention you've given the financing process will insure you receive your loan commitment papers within a month. However, if you're rejected, don't get upset. First, remember rejection is a reaction to the facts provided in your application, not a permanent decision. Ask your shepherd why your application was rejected. By law you must be provided with a reason. Once you receive an answer, you can address the deficiency in your application by bringing new facts to their attention. Also, bear in mind that a bank's decision on whether or not to make a loan is based in large part on your ability to meet the monthly payments. That means you can often turn a rejection into an acceptance simply by asking for less money, or for a longer period of time to pay it back. Find out about the appeals procedure, and as soon as you finish a new and improved application package begin the process. Present your appeal not as a debate but as "a request for a reconsideration based on new information." Meanwhile, go back to your mortgage shopping checklists, find another potential lender, and start the application process all over again. Above all, don't give up: There's a lender for every borrower.

Once you do get your commitment papers, don't rush to sign them. These are legally binding documents that need to be studied. Sit down with your attorney and compare the terms and conditions contained in the commitment documents to the information you received over the telephone. If there are discrepancies, contact your shepherd. If not, sign them, make a copy for your records, and deliver them in person to your shepherd. Thank him or her profusely for their efforts. If you have a good contact at a bank, it makes sense to maintain it.

With your financing lined up, you probably think there's nothing left standing between you and the renovated home of your dreams. You're wrong.

Obtaining Copies of Your Credit Report

There are three major credit bureaus, each of which may have credit files on you. In order to properly examine and clean your credit report you need to obtain copies of each credit bureau's file. Unless you've recently been turned down for credit there's a small charge. For complete information on obtaining copies and making corrections, call each credit bureau directly. Here are the addresses and telephone numbers of each:

TRW Credit Data
National Consumer
Relations Center
12606 Greenville Avenue
P.O. Box 749029
Dallas, TX 75374-9029
(212) 235-1200, extension 251

Equifax (also known as CBI)
P.O. Box 4081
Atlanta, GA 30302
(404) 885-8000

Trans Union (East)
P.O. Box 360
Philadelphia, PA 19105
(215) 569-4582

Trans Union (Midwest)
222 South First Street,
Suite 201
Louisville, KY 40202
(502) 584-0121

Trans Union (West)
P.O. Box 3110
Fullerton, CA 92634
(714) 738-3800

FIRST AND SECOND MORTGAGE SHOPPING CHECKLIST

The following worksheet should be used when calling lenders for information on home-equity loans, home-equity lines of credit, and refinancing mortgages. Make photocopies of these pages and use one set for each bank (more if they have more than three plans). Don't feel pressured to skip any lines. In order to be able to compare and select the loan that's right for you, you'll need to fill in every appropriate blank. (Terms marked with an asterisk are explained in the glossary at the end of the chapter.)

	Plan A	Plan B	Plan C
Name of lender			
Telephone number			
Name of contact			
Address			

	Plan A	Plan B	Plan C
Adjustable-rate loans			
Interest rate			
Adjustment period*			
Index*			
Adjustment period cap*			
Lifetime cap*			
Convertible? Yes or No*			
If yes, when?			
And what's the cost?			
Loan term			
Points*			
Origination fee*			
Loan to value ratio—LTV*			
Average percentage rate*			
Fixed-rate loans			
Interest rate			
Points			
Origination fee			
Loan term			
LTV			
Average percentage rate			

All loans

Nonincome verification*　　———————　　———————　　———————

Nonstandard LTV*　　———————　　———————　　———————

Debt to income ratio　　———————　　———————　　———————

Application fee　　———————　　———————　　———————

Appraisal fee　　———————　　———————　　———————

Credit check fee　　———————　　———————　　———————

Credit bureau used　　———————　　———————　　———————

Bank attorney fee　　———————　　———————　　———————

Prepayment penalty*　　———————　　———————　　———————

　If yes, when?　　———————　　———————　　———————

　And what's the cost?　　———————　　———————　　———————

Response time　　———————　　———————　　———————

Length of commitment　　———————　　———————　　———————

Commitment renewable　　———————　　———————　　———————

　If yes, same rate?　　———————　　———————　　———————

　New rate?　　———————　　———————　　———————

Rate lock-in　　———————　　———————　　———————

　If yes, when?　　———————　　———————　　———————

　And what's the cost?　　———————　　———————　　———————

Special programs　　———————　　———————　　———————

Preferred benefits　　———————　　———————　　———————

Documentation Required

Fees　　———————　　———————　　———————

Pay stub　　———————　　———————　　———————

Tax returns	_____	_____	_____
Profit and loss or income statements	_____	_____	_____
Contract of sale	_____	_____	_____
Offering plan, etc.	_____	_____	_____
Building financials	_____	_____	_____
Other	_____	_____	_____

GLOSSARY OF TERMS USED IN MORTGAGE-SHOPPING CHECKLIST

adjustment period the frequency with which the interest rate will be adjusted.

adjustment period cap a ceiling on the amount the interest rate of an adjustable-rate mortgage can increase at any one time.

average percentage rate the actual amount of interest that a borrower will effectively pay. This number, which lenders are legally bound to provide, is the single best means for judging loan plans since it allows dissimilar plans to be compared with each other.

convertible? yes or no? whether or not the adjustable-rate mortgage can be converted into a fixed-rate mortgage. In some loan plans, after a certain period of time (often three to five years), the interest rate ceases being flexible and must be negotiated into a fixed rate.

index a measure of relative value to which the adjustable-rate mortgage is linked in order to determine the interest rate. Two of the most common are the Federal Home Loan Bank Board's national average mortgage rate and the U.S. Treasury bill rate.

loan-to-value (LTV) ratio the maximum percentage of a property's value that a bank will offer in a mortgage.

Most banks prefer to loan only up to 80 percent of value for first mortgages and up to 75 percent on second or refinanced mortgages.

nonincome verification   an option in which the bank does not require objective verification of an applicant's income. Often used by self-employed individuals whose actual income may not be reflected by their income tax returns. Under this option the lender may not be willing to commit to financing 80 percent of the property's value.

nonstandard loan-to-value (LTV) ratio   an option in which the bank may be willing to lend more than 80 percent of the value of the property being purchased. Sometimes this service is provided for preferred customers, or by special arrangement with a developer who may be picking up some of the bank's costs.

origination fee   a charge for starting financing of a home mortgage that is allegedly used to cover the lender's administrative costs in processing the loan.

points   percentage points of interest. In mortgages, this term refers to an up-front charge of a certain number of interest points levied by some lenders. This reduces the monthly payment on the mortgage, but increases the amount required at closing.

preferred benefits   some banks offer preferred customers (someone who has been a sizable depositor for a lengthy period of time) special benefits, such as waiver of certain fees, and a less stringent or time-consuming approval process.

prepayment penalty   extra money that must be paid if a loan is paid off early, which allegedly compensates the lender for paperwork and lost interest.

CHAPTER 11

Avoiding and Resolving Problems During and After the Job

People who are only good with
hammers see every problem as a nail.
—ABRAHAM MASLOW

The best way to minimize the problems on your job is to avoid doing things that could lead to them. Just by doing everything I've discussed throughout this book you'll have gone a long way to cutting down the possibilities of problems cropping up.

Having done your homework on affordability early in the process, and getting a fixed- or budget-price agreement with your general contractor should eliminate potential money problems. That complete set of plans and specifications, which you lived with and adapted prior to bidding, should keep additions to a minimum. And since you hammered out the prices for these add-ons while negotiating your contract, you'll know exactly what you're getting into if you do request them. (If you didn't agree on a price for a particular type of extra work that the general contractor suggests or you think you might like, make sure to ask how much it will cost before okaying it. Many times, homeowners ask "is it possible to . . ." "would it be okay to . . ." or "will it delay the job to . . ." but forget to ask the price.)

Since you spent so much time selecting your general contractor, questions of incompetency and financial insolvency shouldn't be a factor. But that doesn't mean something won't happen to delay your job or drive it over budget. In fact, you should probably count on something unexpected happening.

There could be a freak hailstorm, which keeps the crew from working for a couple of days. The carpenters might discover a rotten beam or sill that needs replacing. Your general contractor might get pneumonia. The building inspectors could be perpetually late, delaying work from progressing. Or you might lose your temper.

Don't laugh off this last possibility. It happens all the time, and in a way, it's understandable. Your house, for all intents and purposes, is no longer your own. You'll either have turned it over to the general contractor and her crew entirely, or will be sharing it with them. Their lunches will be in your refrigerator. They'll be tracking mud through your hallway. That means you'll be on edge throughout the project. And once you start writing checks, you'll have the uncomfortable sense you're paying a lot of money for the privilege of having your house taken over and demolished.

Your natural response to all this will be to remain vigilant against any waste or delays. One day you'll stop by during your lunch hour and find workmen resting, eating lunch, or just leaning on a shovel. You'll want to scream at them to get back to work. Hold your tongue. Just because they're taking a break when you arrive don't assume they have been goofing off all day long. Everyone needs to take breaks during the day. A construction worker leaning on a shovel is the equivalent of an office worker getting a cup of coffee.

I'll never forget how one client of mine stopped by the site during the day and began yelling at a workman who was taking a break. His anger and frustration got the better of him and he insisted the general contractor get rid of the laborer. The general contractor protested mildly, but gave in. Afterwards, the general contractor took me aside and explained that the laborer my client yelled at and had him fire was far and away the best worker on the site. When I asked why the general contractor didn't put up more of a fight, he correctly noted: "The homeowner is the boss—he's signing the checks."

The natural flow of renovation projects can also lead to frustration. The first third of any job moves very quickly. Demolition is fairly easy, it makes a huge impression, and it is pretty inexpensive. In what seems like no time, and for very little money, the crew has gotten your home ready for the new work. But then things begin to slow. Rough framing and foundation work are slower and more expensive than demolition, but still quite impressive, quick, and affordable. Then things start to change. The job starts slowing down and getting expensive. Finish work takes longer, costs more, and is much less noticeable than demolition or rough framing. It seems like the money being spent is out of proportion to the amount of progress on the job. And as the job moves ahead the work gets slower and the costs get steeper. The resulting frustration gets the better of some homeowners.

Even if you keep your frustration under wraps, your enthusiasm could lead to problems. Curiosity not only can kill the cat, it can annoy the craftsman. Even if you find construction work fascinating, and would love to learn how to do things, don't follow craftsmen around asking for tips. You're paying them to do a job, not to give you lessons. They probably would never directly say you're annoying them, but their anger will be reflected in their work. Remember you're the chief executive officer of this project, not the foreman. Don't make a nuisance of yourself. If you have general questions, ask them of the general contractor. If there are a couple of specific things you'd like to ask a particular craftsman, run them by the general contractor first, and find out when would be the best time to talk to the subcontractor.

Don't take this urging to be diplomatic to mean that I think you should become a supplicant to the general contractor and the subs. By all means show up at the job whenever you'd like. In fact, I'd encourage you to visit at irregular times just to keep the general contractor and her crew on their toes. Your presence should be felt, but subtly. From Stalin through Saddam Hussein, dictators have insisted on their pictures being present almost everywhere. The portrait hanging on the wall acts as a reminder: It says that while the dictator may not be there physically, their power is everywhere. By showing up at the job site now and then you can have the same effect. But don't act like an inspector general while visiting. Explain that you were in the neighborhood and decided to stop by. No one will believe this, but it sounds better than saying you wanted to keep them on their toes. If you see anything that troubles you, make a mental note of it, and ask the general contractor about it before you leave. What initially appears to be a mistake or problem could just be a temporary step in a process you don't fully understand. If it turns out you did spot a problem, make a note of it when you get back to your car. Keep a list of any problems and mistakes you discover. This will become your checklist when it comes time to release your final payment. Let the general contractor know that you won't consider the job completed, and won't make your last payment, until all these problems are addressed.

I don't mean to give you the impression that if you control your temper and enthusiasm, all will go well. It may, and then again, it may not. There really are certain things that are beyond your control. For instance: You're not paying building inspectors' salaries—at least not directly—so you have little control over their punctuality. And complaining to their superiors probably isn't a bright idea. In many cases, visits by building inspectors are perfunctory. The inspector probably knows the general contractor and the subcontractors—he may even be a friend. If he knows the past work of the general contractor and her crew to have been up to snuff, his inspection may be a mere formality. But if you come down on him for showing up late and delaying your job, a ten-minute once-over could turn into a daylong, minute examination, perhaps revealing some minor matters which need to be redone. In other words, let sleeping dogs lie.

While I'm on the subject, let me tell you a little bit about building departments. If you live in a major metropolitan area and hire an architect to draw up your plans and file the papers, that may be the last time you ever need to deal with the building department. Most big city building departments are overworked and understaffed. They simply don't have the manpower to inspect every building project thoroughly. If the plans submitted to a big city building department bear the signature of a licensed architect, perhaps a local one known to the officials, they're often accepted without question. In fact, in some major cities, if a licensed architect has signed the plans they won't even bother inspecting the job. In smaller cities, suburban towns, and rural villages, on the other hand, you can expect building department inspectors to become regular visitors to your job site. They'll be stopping by at various times to place their seals of approval on the work already done. Once they've given the okay, the job can continue.

Because filing plans with the local building department can invite unavoidable delays many homeowners are tempted to do an end run around the rules, and have the work done without the necessary permits. I think that's a terrible idea, and not just because I'm an attorney. First, and most importantly, it's illegal. Second, the building codes are there to insure your work is done properly and your home is safe. And third, work done on the sly will come back to haunt you. When it comes time to sell your home, the attorney for the buyers will undoubtedly discover your additions are illegal and the certificate of occupancy (a form issued by the municipality describing your home exactly and stating how it can and cannot be used) for your home is invalid. That could break the deal. If you ever need to make an insurance claim for damage to your property, your insurer may refuse to pay, and cancel your policy, if it discovers your certificate of occupancy isn't up to date. In other words, you will eventually be found out.

I first began my legal practice in Suffolk County, New York. At that time it was an expansive suburb, considered on the fringes of the New York City metropolitan area. Residents had a touch of the pioneering spirit. It was common for homeowners to have pools built in their backyards without informing the local building department. After all, they thought, if county officials couldn't see the pool from the street how would they ever find out? Eventually, word got out and the building department wised up. It hired a private plane to fly over the county. An airborne inspector duly noted the locations of all the illegal pools and the homeowners faced fines in addition to tax increases.

Building department bureaucracy isn't the only unavoidable thing that could delay your job. Let's say there's a freak hailstorm that keeps the framing crew from working for a day. That could easily throw off the whole job schedule. No one is to blame for it, so you probably have no recourse. Similarly, if the carpenters discover a steel girder inside a wall that needs to be removed, you may have no choice but to swallow the delay and the added costs incurred.

That doesn't mean you need to swallow every delay or cost overrun. Your general contractor should know what the normal weather conditions are, and what problems are likely to surface, and should have taken them into account when preparing her bid and schedule. You didn't try to hammer away at her overhead and profit, so she has no excuse for not providing herself with a big enough cushion. Try to enlist your planning and supervisory professional as an ally in these situations. Ask them whether or not a particular problem or delay should reasonably have been foreseen. If they agree with you, you're on very strong ground. But don't be surprised if their response is less than satisfying.

The professionals involved in home renovation, whether they are architects or iron workers, have become accustomed to delays and cost overruns. None of them believe a job can actually be completed on time and at

budget, let alone early and for less money than was anticipated. Home renovation is sort of like Hollywood in that
regard: If a film wraps early and for less money than anticipated, the studio executives wonder what's wrong with
it. The same holds true for renovation projects. Everyone,
but you, is just waiting for something to go wrong. It almost becomes a self-fulfilling prophecy—they look for
something to delay them and run up the tab.

By following the process laid out in this book you've
done everything humanly possible to avoid problems. But
if one arises during the project, you'll face an unpleasant
choice: battle your general contractor over who should pay
for it, and you risk alienating her and the subcontractors
and having them take out their frustration on your house;
cave in and agree to pay more, and your budget is shot. My
suggestion is to look for a middle ground. Offer to extend
the completion date, but ask the general contractor to bear
the added cost. Or suggest splitting the cost overrun. Even
though you have a contract with a budget price, you don't
want an angry, potentially bankrupt general contractor
working—or perhaps not working—on your house. It will
cost you twice as much to hire another general contractor
to come in and finish the job. Bite the bullet, compromise,
and take solace from the pleasure and comfort the renovations will bring to your life.

Problems that develop after the job has been "completed" are another matter entirely. Home renovation
work isn't an exact science. While good craftsmen are ex-
acting in their work, houses themselves, particularly older
ones, are not exact constructions. They breathe and settle,
expand and contract. Things that once were level or plumb
shift. Because of this, there's often a period after a renovation project during which the bugs need to be taken out

of the job. That's one reason why you made sure to retain 10 percent of each payment, including the last, until thirty days after the job has been deemed complete by your supervisory professional. Your 10 percent retainage and their personal guarantee is hopefully enough leverage to insure the general contractor and her crew will return to iron out any problems.

But sometimes, general contractors and homeowners differ as to what is a problem and what isn't. Or more to the point, what is the general contractor's fault and what isn't. The general contractor may claim the problem is the manufacturer's responsibility, or that it was inherent in the plans and specifications. In fact, she may just not want to come back. She could have lined up other jobs, or perhaps she wants to start her vacation. And sometimes, if a job hasn't been a very profitable one, they may just be annoyed. Stick to your guns. You have the leverage—the 10 percent—and the law on your side.

First, decide exactly what you want the general contractor to do. Would you prefer she send someone back to fix the problem, or would you rather have someone else do the work, and just deduct the cost from your retainage? Unless you had a personality clash with the general contractor, I'd suggest you let them do the work. Discuss the matter with the general contractor. Don't get angry. Simply explain what you would like done.

If you don't get satisfaction, or find yourself getting nasty, end the conversation. Contact your supervisory professional and ask them to mediate the problem. Very often disputes are easier to resolve if they are handled within the trade. If your supervisory professional can't settle the matter, contact either the National Association of Home Builders, or the authority which licensed the general contractor. These groups have leverage with the general contractor, since they can revoke her membership or license. In most cases the association will take action within a couple of weeks.

In the unlikely event the problem is still unresolved, exercise your right under the contract to bring the matter to the American Arbitration Association. This well-respected group has offices in most cities. Hearings are usually scheduled within a month, and a decision will be reached no later than a month after the hearing—usually quicker. The "loser" pays the association a fee of $150 and a percentage of the settlement. If, heaven forbid, your general contractor has become financially insolvent in the interim, contact your area's consumer protection agency. Many municipalities and states funnel a portion of the monies received in licensing fees into a refund account for wronged consumers. They may be able to give you the money if your general contractor can't. Be aware that the maximum refund they can provide may not be enough to cover your loss—but something is better than nothing.

CHAPTER 12

The Big Picture

—

> 'Mid pleasures and palaces though we
> may roam,
> Be it ever so humble, there's no place
> like home.
>
> —JOHN HOWARD PAYNE

There is no denying that the home renovation process is fraught with potential problems. More complaints are made to the Better Business Bureau about home contractors than any other business. The only other consumer transaction that combines equal parts finance and emotion and wraps them up in an incredibly complex process is arranging a funeral—but at least that is over within a week. A disastrous home renovation can linger on for months, even years if it becomes tied up in litigation.

But by following the strategies and tactics outlined in

this book you can, I believe, eliminate the chances of that happening to you.

By realizing that home renovations are too difficult and too important to do yourself, you will open the door to a truly professional job.

By examining your needs and wants and comparing them to the estimated cost of home renovation projects, you'll decide whether or not renovation is a good idea for you.

By carefully studying your local market—with the help of a real estate appraiser and real estate broker—you will determine whether or not your proposed renovation makes financial sense.

By balancing that information with a sense of how long you'll actually be living in the home, and how much the proposed renovation will improve your lifestyle, you'll decide whether or not to have the work done.

By carefully going over your personal finances, deciding what you are willing to give up in exchange for a renovated home, and studying the financing alternatives, you'll calculate exactly how much you can afford to spend.

By carefully scheduling your project to coincide with the slow period for the home renovation industry, you'll insure you get the most for your money.

By hiring a professional to draft a set of comprehensive plans and specifications and supervise the construction, you'll guarantee that the work will be up to standards.

By selecting the right type and size general contractors to bid on your job you'll make it possible to compare the bids accurately.

By investigating general contractors and judging the work of their subcontractors you'll know that the team you're hiring is made up of professional, financially solvent, and reliable craftsmen.

By carefully analyzing the individual bids you'll be able to select those most likely to do the best job.

By drafting and signing an equitable and enforceable contract with your general contractor, formalizing the terms of your relationship and the costs of your job, you'll have done everything possible to insure the work is done on time and within budget.

By cleaning your credit report, comparison shopping, and bypassing the scoring system you'll find and qualify for the best financing available.

And by stepping back, relaxing, and letting the trained professionals do their jobs, you'll minimize the chances for disputes and problems.

I'll grant you that the plan I've laid out is time-consuming, requires insight and self-examination, and may initially cost more than the standard approach to home renovation. But the standard approach to home renovation has, in the majority of cases, resulted in dissatisfied homeowners. My plan puts you in charge of the process, minimizes the risks, and maximizes the potential rewards. The slightly higher cost of enlisting professional help—such as appraisers, real estate brokers, architects, home inspectors, and attorneys—is more than made up for by the help, assurance, and comfort their expertise and advice can provide, not to mention their ability to save you from potential disasters.

Home renovation should be, and can be, an exhilarating and rewarding process. You're increasing the value of your single most important asset, the asset which will become the source of all the other major financial moves you make in your life. You're putting your money into arguably the safest long-term investment in America—residential real estate—and retaining full control over that investment. Your investment in a renovation not only yields financial benefits, but lifestyle ones as well; renovations are the only investments where you really can have your cake and eat it too.

But perhaps more importantly, when you choose to renovate a home you're making a statement. You're turning a house into a home. You're saying "I belong here." You're putting down roots. In the end, you're making a statement about permanence. And in today's chaotic and confusing world, where trends appear and disappear, where everyone has fifteen minutes of fame, where enemies become friends and friends become enemies, that's quite a powerful statement.

Appendix

SAMPLE CUSTOM CONTRACT BETWEEN
HOMEOWNER AND GENERAL CONTRACTOR

AGREEMENT made as of this _____ day of _____
by and between _____
having its principal office at _____
("Contractor") and _____
_____ ("Owner").

RECITALS

Owner owns the land and the single-family dwelling
which now exists thereon commonly known as _____
_____ (the "Premises"). Contractor represents that he
is a licensed contractor and is engaged in and proficient at
the business of renovating homes and buildings. Owner
and Contractor have agreed that Contractor will _____
_____
_____
_____ together with other work as more
fully set forth below. Contractor will perform all of the
work and make all the improvements on the terms and
conditions and pursuant to the plans and specifications as
more fully described below and attached hereto.

NOW, THEREFORE, THE PARTIES AGREE AS FOLLOWS

1. Scope of the Construction Project

The Contractor shall demolish those portions of the _____ as reflected on the attached architectural plans and shall provide all labor, materials, supervision, tools, and knowledge to construct and shall construct _____ and perform the other work in and about the existing residence as shown on those plans in a good and workmanlike manner and strictly in compliance with the terms and conditions set forth below and the specifications and plans attached hereto.

2. Time

The Contractor agrees to commence the demolition and construction of the project no later than _____, _____ (the "Commencement Date") and to fully complete all of the construction on or before _____, _____ (the "Completion Date") by which time the Contractor shall have completed all construction referred to below and shall have obtained a final, amended certificate of occupancy for the use of the modified residence as a legal single-family residence together with all other necessary permits, licenses and other documents required to use the Premises, as modified, as a legal single family dwelling. The time limits stated herein are of the essence and the Contractor shall expedite the work and achieve Substantial Completion within the designated time period. The date of "Substantial Completion" of the Contractor's work shall be the later to occur of the following dates (i) the date the Construction Manager (as designated below) has certified that construction is sufficiently complete so that the Owner can occupy or use the premises as a legal single-family dwelling; or (ii) the Contractor shall have obtained the final certificate of occupancy.

If the Contractor is delayed at any time in the progress of his work by changes ordered in the work by the Owner, labor disputes, fire, unusual delay in transportation outside the Contractor's control, adverse weather conditions not reasonably anticipated, unavoidable casualties or any causes beyond the Contractor's control, then the time in which the Contractor shall have completed the work specified herein shall be extended for an appropriately reasonable time not to exceed forty-five (45) days.

3. Contract Documents

The Contract Documents consist of this Agreement, the Specifications annexed hereto and initialed by the parties, the architectural blueprints and drawings pages _____ through _____ (including general notes) all dated _____ , _____ and prepared by _____ of _____ _____ .

The intent of the Contract Documents specified above is to include all items necessary for the proper execution and completion of the work to be performed by the Contractor. Any work not covered by or specified within the Contract Documents will not be required unless it is consistent therewith and reasonably inferable therefrom as being necessary to produce the intended results.

By executing this Agreement, the Contractor represents that he has visited the work site, familiarized himself with the local conditions under which the work is to be performed, estimated the cost of the job and has entered into this Agreement with full and complete knowledge thereof.

The work to be performed by the Contractor comprises the completed construction required by this Agreement and the other Contract Documents and includes all labor necessary to produce the construction, and all materials and equipment incorporated or to be incorporated in or used to complete that construction.

4. Payments

(i) The Owner shall pay to the Contractor for the performance of the work specified herein, subject to any additions and/or deductions as covered by a work change orders prepared by the Contractor and signed by the Owner, the total contract sum of $_____.

(ii) Attached to this Agreement is schedule "A," captioned "Schedule of Payments and Construction Progress." That schedule specifies the various stages of the demolition and construction of the building that the Contractor will construct for the Owner. The Owner has selected ___

_____ to act as the Owner's construction manager (the "Construction Manager"). When the Contractor has completed each of the stages listed on schedule "A," he shall promptly notify the Owner and the Construction Manager of the completion of that stage of the work and request the Construction Manager to visit the job site and inspect the work performed during that stage. The Construction Manager shall inspect the job site and work performed within forty-eight (48) hours of receiving such notice of completion from the Contractor. The Construction Manager shall, after receiving such notice, inspect the work to ascertain that the work for that stage has been performed in strict and full compliance with the terms of this contract and with the plans, drawings, and specifications attached hereto. If the Construction Manager finds that the work either has not been performed in compliance with the specifications, drawings, and plans or in any other way is not acceptable to the Construction Manager, the Construction Manager shall notify the Contractor in writing of any such deficiencies. Upon the receipt of such a notice of any deficiencies, if there be any, the Contractor shall promptly remedy the defective or unacceptable work or complete the work in the manner as specified by the Construction Manager. Once the work has been completed or changed as required, the Contractor shall promptly notify the Construction Manager and ask that he reinspect the work at that time. If the work has been completed or modified as required, and then complies with the terms of this agreement and with the drawings, plans, and specifications attached hereto, the Construction Manager shall certify to the Contractor and to the Owner that the work has been performed in strict and full compliance with this contract and with the drawings, plans, and specifications attached hereto. The Owner agrees to make each progress payment within five (5) days of receipt from the Construction Manager of notice that the work performed during that stage has been completed. The Contractor shall not be obligated to continue any further work if a progress payment is not timely made after certification by the Construction Manager.

It shall not be a cause or justification of Contractor ceasing any further work on the project that Contractor has not received a progress payment if the work for that stage has not yet been approved by the Construction Manager or Owner.

(iii) The final payment as specified on schedule "A" constitutes the entire unpaid balance of the agreed-upon contract sum and shall be paid by the Owner to the Contractor when all of the work as specified in this Agreement and on the drawings, plans, and specifications attached hereto has been completed, a final certificate of occupancy for use of the premises as a single-family dwelling has been obtained by the Contractor and delivered to the Owner and the Construction Manager has issued his final certificate for payment. Final payment shall not be due until the Contractor has delivered to the Owner a complete release of all liens arising out of this Contract or receipt in full covering all labor, materials, and equipment for which a lien could be filed, or shall have delivered to the Owner a bond reasonably satisfactory to the Owner indemnifying the Owner against any such liens. If any lien remains unsatisfied after all payments are made, the Contractor shall refund to the Owner all monies the Owner may be compelled to pay in discharging such lien or liens, including all costs and reasonable attorneys fees incurred.

(iv) The making of a final payment by the Owner to the Contractor shall constitute a waiver of all claims by the Owner except those arising from (a) unsettled liens; (b) faulty or defective work appearing after Substantial Completion; (c) failure of the work to comply with the requirements of the Contract Documents; or (d) the terms of any special warranties required by the Contract Documents. The acceptance of final payment by the Contractor shall constitute a waiver of all claims by the Contractor against the Owner except those previously made in writing and identified by the Contractor as unsettled at the time final application for payment is made to the Owner.

(v) The parties recognize that some of the items of materials purchased by the Contractor may be taxable. To the extent any portion of the monies paid by Owner to Contractor are for sales taxes, the parties agree that Owner shall be entitled to the tax deduction. Contractor will supply Owner, upon request, copies of all bills, invoices, receipts, etc.

5. Work Change Orders

The Owner, without invalidating this Agreement, may order changes in the work consisting of additions, deletions, or modifications. All such change of work orders shall be discussed with the Contractor and shall be in form prepared by the Contractor and signed by the Owner. All work change orders shall be for fixed amounts, fixed at the time the work change order is approved by the Owner, or computed as follows, at the Owner's option, if the amount of the charge is not fixed:

(i) Labor shall be charged at a fixed amount as specified in the work change order or at the rate of $_____ per hour per workman; and

(ii) All material shall be at the fixed amount as specified in the work change order or at 10% above the Contractor's cost, the Contractor to supply copies of paid invoices to the Owner.

At the time any work change order is prepared by the Contractor and signed by the Owner, that work change order shall specify the amount of additional time that will be required by the Contractor to complete the project and the Completion Date shall be adjusted accordingly. If no time is specified in the work change order, the Completion Date shall not be extended.

The Owner shall pay to Contractor at the time of signing a work change order 50% of the cost of that change and shall pay to the Contractor one-half of the remaining balance at such time as the Construction Manager shall certify that the work covered by the work change order has been completed. The remaining balance of the cost of that work change order shall be paid to the Contractor at the time the final payment, specified on schedule "A," is made to the Contractor.

6. *Obligations of Contractor*

(i) The Contractor shall supervise and direct the work, using his best skill and attention and he shall be solely responsible for all construction means, methods, techniques, sequences, and procedures and for coordinating all portions of the work under the Contract.

(ii) Unless otherwise specifically provided in the Contract Documents, the Contractor shall provide and pay for all labor, materials, equipment, tools, construction equipment and machinery, water, heat, utilities, transportation, and other facilities and services necessary for the proper execution and completion of the work, whether temporary or permanent and whether or not incorporated or to be incorporated in the work.

(iii) The Contractor shall at all times enforce strict discipline and good order among his employees and shall not employ on the job any unfit person or anyone not skilled in the task assigned to him.

(iv) The Contractor warrants to the Owner that all materials and equipment incorporated in the work will be new unless otherwise specified, and that all work will be good quality, free from faults and defects and in conformance with the Contract Documents and applicable building codes. All work not conforming to these requirements may be considered defective.

(v) Unless otherwise provided in the Contract Documents, the Contractor shall pay all sales, consumer, use, and other similar taxes which are legally enacted at the time bids are received, and shall secure the building permit and all other permits, licenses, and inspections necessary for the proper execution and completion of the work.

(vi) The Contractor shall give all notices and comply with all laws, ordinances, rules, regulations, and lawful orders of any public authority bearing on the performance of the work, and shall promptly notify the Owner if the drawings and specifications are at variance therewith.

(vii) The Contractor shall be responsible to the Owner for the acts and omissions of his employees, subcontractors and their agents and employees, and other persons performing any of the work under a contract with the Contractor.

(viii) The Contractor shall review, approve, and submit all shop drawings, product data, and samples required by the Contract Documents. The work shall be in accordance with approved and signed submittal.

(ix) The Contractor at all times shall keep the premises free from accumulation of waste materials or rubbish caused by his operations. At the completion of the work he shall remove all his waste materials and rubbish from and about the premises as well as his tools, construction equipment, machinery, and surplus materials.

(x) To the fullest extent permitted by law, the Contractor shall indemnify and hold harmless the Owner and the Construction Manager and their agents and employees from and against all claims, damages, losses, and expenses, including but not limited to attorney's fees arising out of or resulting from the performance of the work, provided that any such claim, damage, loss, or expense (1) is attributable to bodily injury, sickness, disease or death, or to injury to or destruction of tangible property (other than the work itself) including the loss of use resulting therefrom, and (2) is caused in whole or in part by any negligent act or omission of the Contractor, any subcontractor, anyone directly or indirectly employed by any of them or anyone for whose acts any of them may be liable, regardless of whether or not it is caused in part by a party indemnified hereunder. Such obligation shall not be construed to negate, abridge, or otherwise reduce any other right or obligation of indemnity which would otherwise exist as to any party or person described in this paragraph. In any and all claims against the Owner or any of their agents or employees by any employee of the Contractor, any subcontractor, anyone directly or indirectly employed by any of them or anyone for whose acts any of them may be liable, the indemnification obligation under this paragraph shall not be limited in any way by any limitation on the amount or type of damages, compensation, or benefits payable by or for the Contractor or any subcontractor under workers' or workmen's compensation acts, disability benefit acts, or other employee benefit acts.

7. *Protection of Persons and Property*

The Contractor shall be responsible for initiating, maintaining, and supervising all safety precautions and programs in connection with the work. He shall take all reasonable precautions for the safety of, and shall provide all reasonable protection to prevent damage, injury, or loss to (1) all employees on the work and other persons who may be affected thereby, (2) all the work and all materials and equipment to be incorporated therein, and (3) other property at the site or adjacent thereto. He shall give all notices and comply with all applicable laws, ordinances, rules, regulations, and orders of any public authority bearing on the safety of persons and property and their protection from damage, injury, or loss. The Contractor shall promptly remedy all damage or loss to any property caused in whole or in part by the Contractor, any subcontractor, or anyone directly or indirectly employed by any of them, or by anyone for whose acts any of them may be liable, except damage or loss attributable to the acts or omissions of the Owner or anyone directly or indirectly employed by them or by anyone for whose acts they may be liable, and not attributable to the fault or negligence of the Contractor.

8. *Insurance*

(i) The Owner shall, at the Owner's sole cost and expense, adequately insure the building and the work and materials used in the building in the names of the Owner and the Contractor, as their interests may appear, against loss by fire, with extended coverage.

(ii) The Contractor shall, at the Contractor's sole cost and expense, obtain and maintain insurance required under the workmen's compensation law of _____ and shall provide and keep in full force for the benefit of the Owner, general public liability insurance, protecting the Owner against any and all liability or claims or liability arising out of, occasioned by, or resulting from any accident, happening or otherwise in or about the premises for injuries to any person or persons, for limits of not less than one million dollars for injuries to one person in any one accident or occurrence, and for loss or damage to property of any person or persons for not less than $500,000.00; and will save, hold and keep harmless and indemnify the Owner from and for all claims and liability for losses to persons or to any adjacent lands and property which may have been caused by the Contractor or Contractor's workmen, agents, employees, invitees, or licensees.

9. Permits, Licenses and Approval

The Contractor shall take whatever action is necessary and shall obtain all building permits or approvals as required by the local municipality, governmental agency, or public authority having jurisdiction thereof, or as may be necessary or required under any law, ordinance, or regulation including demolition and construction of any of the building and the work called for hereunder, the cost for which shall be borne by the Contractor. The Contractor agrees to conform with all statutory and municipal laws and regulations, including _____ Building Code, affecting the work, the buildings, and the premises.

The Contractor shall deliver certificate of insurance to the Owner prior to the commencement of any of the work specified herein.

The Owner and the Contractor hereby waive all rights one may have against the other for damages caused by fire or other perils to the extent such damages are covered and reimbursed by insurance.

10. Delay; Liquidated Damages

If the work to be performed by Contractor hereunder is not completed by the Completion Date, as same may have been extended pursuant to any work change orders, the Owner shall be entitled to damages. The damages shall be at the rate of $_____ for each day beyond the Completion Date (as it may be extended under the terms of this Agreement) that the work is not fully completed. It is agreed that this amount fixed as damages is reasonable considering the losses Owner will suffer if there is a delay. The parties have agreed to choose this amount as the liquidated amount of Owner's anticipated damages because it is difficult for the parties to determine exactly the amount of damages that may be caused by the Contractor's delay.

11. Maintenance of Work Site

The Contractor shall continuously maintain adequate protection of the work, materials, the premises, and the adjacent property from injury or loss by reason of the Contractor's operations hereunder and shall make good and replace any such damage or loss and shall take proper, adequate, and necessary precautions for the safety of the public and shall keep the premises free from accumulation of waste, rubbish, and surplus materials. At the completion of the work and before being entitled to the final payment of any monies which may be due hereunder, the Contractor shall remove all waste, rubbish, tools, equipment, scaffolding, and surplus materials and shall leave the premises "broom clean" or its equivalent.

12. Subcontractors

Before any work shall be commenced by the Contractor, Contractor shall deliver to Owner a list, in writing, specifying the names of each of the subcontractors to be used by Contractor for each of the principal portions of the work to be performed hereunder. The Contractor shall not employ any subcontractor to whom the Owner or the Construction Manager may have a reasonable objection. All contracts between the Contractor and the various subcontractors shall require each subcontractor, to the extent of the work to be performed by that subcontractor, to be bound to the Contractor by the terms of the Contract Documents and to assume toward the Contractor all the obligations and responsibilities which the Contractor, by these contract documents, assumes toward the Owner.

13. Mechanics Liens

Within forty-five days of the filing against the premises of any mechanics' lien by any subcontractor or materialmen employed by the Contractor, the Contractor shall discharge such lien of record with adequate surety in an amount as fixed by a justice of the _____ _____ Court, ____ County. In the event the Contractor does not timely discharge any such mechanics' liens of record, the Owner may do so and the Contractor shall reimburse the Owner for the cost of discharging every such lien, including reasonable attorneys fees incurred in connection therewith.

Prior to the time that Owner shall make any payment to Contractor as a progress payment set forth on schedule "A," provided such payment reflects the completion of all work by any particular subcontractor (or materialman), the Contractor shall obtain from such subcontractor (or in the case of a materialman, from the materialman) a statement, substantially in the form as attached as exhibit "B" which shall be signed by the subcontractor or materialman and delivered to Owner or Owner's representative prior to the time that Owner shall be obligated to make that particular progress payment to the Contractor.

14. Arbitration

In the event there is any controversy or claim arising out of, or relating to this Agreement or the breach thereof, such controversy or claim shall be settled by arbitration in _____ _____ in accordance with the rules then obtaining of the American Arbitration Association, and the parties agree that judgment upon any award rendered by the arbitrator(s) may be entered in any court having jurisdiction thereof. In addition, the parties agree that, in the event of arbitration, the prevailing party (which shall be defined as the party in whose favor a money or other judgment is awarded) shall be entitled to recover from the other party all of the costs and expenses incurred by the prevailing party in connection with the arbitration and any subsequent enforcement action arising therefrom, including reasonable attorneys fees.

15. Warranty

The Contractor warranties that all of its work to be performed by it in accordance with this Agreement shall be free from any defects in workmanship for a period of two (2) years following the time that the Owner makes the final payment specified on schedule "A" to the Contractor. Notwithstanding the foregoing, however, in the event that any items or materials carrying a manufacturer's warranty (including, but not limited to appliances, windows, plumbing fixtures, etc.) the Contractor shall deliver those warranties to the Owner and the extent of the Contractor's warranty to the Owner with respect to such materials shall be only with respect to the Contractor's work and the Contractor shall not be deemed to be guaranteeing the warranty issued by any manufacturer.

The parties recognize that _____ is the principal of the Contractor. To induce Owner to enter into this Agreement with Contractor, _____ hereby guarantees the foregoing warranty given to the Owner by the Contractor as specified in this paragraph.

16. Miscellaneous

(i) This Agreement and the Contract Documents shall be governed in accordance with the laws of the State of _____.

(ii) This Agreement may not be assigned, by either party, without the prior written consent of the other;

(iii) This Agreement contains all the terms and conditions relating to the subject matter hereof and may not be modified other than by a writing signed by all parties hereto.

(iv) This Agreement shall be binding upon and shall enure to the benefit of the parties, their successors and interests, legal representatives and assigns.

IN WITNESS WHEREOF, the parties hereto have executed this Agreement as of the day and date first above written.

WITNESS:

_____ By:_____

_____   _____

The undersigned, by executing this Agreement, hereby acknowledges his personal guaranty of the warranty set forth in paragraph 14 above.

_____

SAMPLE LETTER CONTRACT BETWEEN
HOMEOWNER
AND DESIGN/PLANNING PROFESSIONAL
FOR CONSTRUCTION MANAGEMENT AND
SUPERVISION

_____

_____
_____
_____
_____
_____

Re: _____

_____
(The "Premises")

Dear _____

You are the _____ that prepared the plans and drawings for the renovation of _____. As you know, I am in the process of negotiating, and will soon sign, a construction contract between myself, as Owner, and _____ as the Contractor. I will provide you with a copy of the executed agreement as soon as it is signed.

I have asked you, and you, in turn, have agreed to act as the Construction Manager as referred to in paragraph 4(ii) of the construction contract.

You have had an opportunity to review a draft or drafts of that construction contract, particularly section 4(ii) which describes the role of the Construction Manager in this renovation project. You have agreed to perform those services, for _____

_____

_____

As we have agreed, you will be responsible for obtaining any and all building permits or approvals required by the local municipality, governmental agencies, or public authority having jurisdiction over the premises and the renovation project to enable to Contractor to begin construction.

I thank you, in advance, for your services as the Construction Manager in that construction contract.

Very truly yours,

_____

Agreed to and Accepted:

_____

INDEX

About the Authors

Stephen Pollan, a nationally known financial consultant, is a personal finance commentator for CNBC/FNN, and has been seen on "Good Morning America" and "Today." He is also the coauthor, with Mark Levine, of *The Business of Living, The Field Guide to Starting a Business, The Field Guide to Home Buying in America,* and *Your Recession Handbook.* Stephen Pollan lives in New York City and Mark Levine lives in Ithaca, New York.